Preface

Mastering Kubernetes has emerged as a cornerstone of modern software development and infrastructure management in recent years. Whether you are a developer looking to streamline your workflows, a DevOps professional aiming to enhance your deployment pipelines, or a systems administrator seeking better scalability and resilience, Kubernetes offers a powerful, open-source solution to orchestrate and manage containerised applications.

This book, Mastering Kubernetes can be both exhilarating and challenging. With its comprehensive ecosystem and rapid evolution, it is essential to understand how Kubernetes works and why it works the way it does. This book is designed to guide you through that journey-from foundational concepts to advanced techniques, equipping you with the knowledge and skills to harness the full potential of Kubernetes in your projects.

The idea for this book was born out of countless interactions with professionals and organisations grappling with the complexities of modern cloud-native technologies. While Kubernetes is an incredibly robust platform, its steep learning curve often deters newcomers and even seasoned engineers. Through this book, my goal is to demystify Kubernetes, presenting its concepts and applications in a way that is both accessible and actionable.

This book is structured to cater to a wide audience. For beginners, it provides clear and concise explanations of core concepts, along with practical examples to build your confidence. It delves into more complex topics such as scaling, security, and troubleshooting for intermediate and advanced readers, offering insights that can help optimise real-world deployments.

Kubernetes is not just a technology; it is a community-driven phenomenon that thrives on collaboration and innovation. As you progress through this book, you will discover not only the technical intricacies of Kubernetes but also its potential to transform how software is developed, deployed, and maintained in the cloud-native era.

This book, Mastering Kubernetes, offers comprehensive learning through diverse formats, including MCQs, true/false, fill-in-the-blanks, match-the-case, short answers, online exam quizzes, and video tutorials. Designed for in-depth understanding and practical application, it ensures an engaging and interactive approach to mastering Kubernetes concepts and real-world implementations.

Thank you for choosing this book as your companion in exploring Kubernetes. Whether you are embarking on your first container orchestration journey or refining your existing expertise, I hope this book serves as a valuable resource and inspires you to achieve new heights in your career and projects.

Happy learning and happy orchestrating.

Table of Contents

Chapter 1 - Introduction to Kubernetes

Learning Objectives

Grasp the basics and benefits of Kubernetes for container orchestration.

Understand key concepts like clusters, nodes, pods, and services.

Learn how Kubernetes simplifies DevOps and supports CI/CD pipelines.

Explore Kubernetes alternatives and their use cases.

Recognise Kubernetes' role in hybrid and multi-cloud environments.

1.1 Overview of Kubernetes

Kubernetes, often abbreviated as K8s, is an open-source container orchestration platform designed to automate the deployment, scaling, and management of containerised applications. Initially developed by Google, Kubernetes is now maintained by the Cloud Native Computing Foundation (CNCF). It has become the de facto standard for managing containerised workloads in cloud-native environments. Kubernetes provides a robust framework for running distributed systems resiliently, handling scaling, failover, deployment patterns, and more.

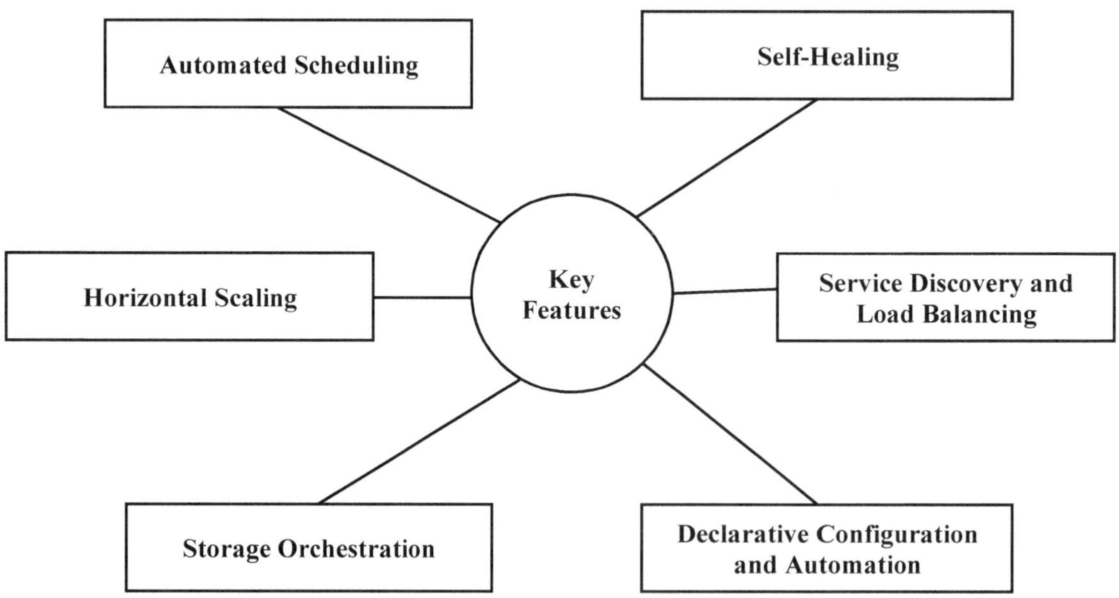

Key Features of Kubernetes

Automated Scheduling: Kubernetes uses advanced scheduling algorithms to efficiently place containers based on resource requirements and constraints, ensuring optimal utilisation of cluster resources.

Self-Healing: The platform continuously monitors the health of nodes and containers. It automatically restarts failed containers, replaces and reschedules containers when nodes fail, and removes containers that do not respond to health checks.

Horizontal Scaling: Applications can be scaled up or down dynamically based on metrics such as CPU and memory usage or custom-defined thresholds.

Service Discovery and Load Balancing: Kubernetes provides DNS-based service discovery, enabling seamless communication between containers. It also balances traffic across containers for improved reliability and performance.

Storage Orchestration: Kubernetes supports automatic provisioning and management of storage resources, allowing applications to use persistent storage from cloud providers like AWS, GCP, and Azure or on-premises solutions.

Declarative Configuration and Automation: Kubernetes manages configurations through declarative YAML or JSON files, enabling Infrastructure as code (IaC) practices and consistent application deployment.

1.2 Why Kubernetes?

The adoption of containerisation and microservices architecture has introduced complexities in managing distributed applications. Kubernetes simplifies these complexities and provides numerous benefits, such as:

Benefits of Kubernetes

Simplifying Operations: Kubernetes automates routine tasks, such as deployment rollouts, scaling, and monitoring, reducing operational overhead.

Ensuring High Availability: By design, Kubernetes provides fault tolerance and ensures application availability through automated failover mechanisms.

Accelerating Development: Developers can focus on writing code without worrying about deployment and scaling, thanks to Kubernetes' abstractions.

Optimizing Resource Usage: Kubernetes dynamically allocates resources to applications, ensuring efficient use of compute, storage, and network resources.

Supporting Hybrid and Multi-Cloud Environments: Kubernetes enables seamless deployment across on-premises, private, and public cloud environments, providing flexibility and avoiding vendor lock-in.

In modern DevOps practices, Kubernetes is an integral part of Continuous Integration and Continuous Delivery (CI/CD) pipelines, enabling fast and reliable application delivery.

1.3 Key Concepts and Terminologies

A strong understanding of Kubernetes requires familiarity with its key components and terminologies. Here are the most important ones:

Cluster: A group of nodes (physical or virtual machines) managed by Kubernetes, which work together to run containerised applications.

Node: An individual machine within the cluster that executes workloads. Nodes can be worker nodes or master nodes (control planes).s

Pod: The smallest deployable unit in Kubernetes, representing one or more tightly coupled containers. Pods share storage, a network, and a specification for running containers.

Service: An abstraction that defines a logical group of Pods and a policy to enable access. Services facilitate communication within and outside the cluster.

Deployment: A higher-level abstraction for managing applications, enabling declarative updates to Pods and ReplicaSets.

ReplicaSet: Ensures a specified number of identical Pod replicas are always running.

Namespace: A virtual cluster within a physical cluster used to isolate resources for different teams or projects.

ConfigMap and **Secret**: Mechanisms for injecting configuration data and sensitive information (e.g., passwords, tokens) into Pods without hardcoding them.

Ingress: A collection of routing rules that manage external HTTP and HTTPS access to services within the cluster.

Kubelet: A lightweight agent that runs on each node, ensuring that containers are running as specified in the Pod definitions.

Kubectl: The command-line interface tool used to interact with Kubernetes clusters.

1.4 Kubernetes Alternatives

While Kubernetes dominates the container orchestration space, several alternatives exist, each suited to specific use cases or preferences. Here are some noteworthy alternatives:

Docker Swarm

Docker Swarm is a native clustering and orchestration tool provided by Docker. It is simpler to set up compared to Kubernetes and integrates seamlessly with Docker's ecosystem. However, it lacks some of Kubernetes' advanced features, such as extensive scaling options and monitoring capabilities.

Apache Mesos/Marathon

Apache Mesos, paired with Marathon, is a resource management platform that can handle both containerised and non-containerized workloads. It is particularly suitable for organisations requiring robust resource allocation for diverse applications.

OpenShift

OpenShift, developed by Red Hat, extends Kubernetes with enterprise-grade features such as integrated CI/CD pipelines, enhanced security, and developer-friendly tools. It is a preferred choice for enterprises seeking a more managed Kubernetes experience.

Nomad

Nomad, by HashiCorp, is a flexible orchestrator that can manage not only containers but also virtual machines and standalone applications. Its simplicity and integration with other HashiCorp tools, such as Consul and Vault, make it appealing for specific use cases.

Rancher

Rancher provides a complete container management solution, including Kubernetes orchestration and additional tools for managing multi-cluster environments. It simplifies cluster operations and offers monitoring, logging, and alerting capabilities.

Amazon ECS (Elastic Container Service)

Amazon ECS is a fully managed container orchestration service by AWS. It is tightly integrated with other AWS services and provides an easy way to deploy containerised applications in the AWS ecosystem. However, it is less flexible for hybrid or multi-cloud deployments compared to Kubernetes.

Azure AKS and Google GKE

While not strictly alternatives, Azure Kubernetes Service (AKS) and Google Kubernetes Engine (GKE) are managed Kubernetes services provided by Azure and Google Cloud, respectively, they reduce the operational complexity of managing Kubernetes clusters and are ideal for organisations already invested in these cloud providers.

Each alternative offers unique advantages and trade-offs. The choice depends on factors such as the organisation's existing infrastructure, scalability needs, and the complexity of the applications being managed.

1.5 Summary

Kubernetes (K8s) is an open-source platform for automating deployment, scaling, and management of containerized applications.

Developed by Google, it is now maintained by the CNCF and is the standard for managing containerized workloads.

Key features include automated scheduling, self-healing, horizontal scaling, service discovery, and declarative configuration.

Kubernetes simplifies the management of microservices and distributed applications, ensuring high availability and efficient resource usage.

It supports hybrid and multi-cloud environments, making it a critical part of modern DevOps and CI/CD pipelines.

Alternatives to Kubernetes include Docker Swarm, OpenShift, Nomad, Rancher, and Amazon ECS, among others.

1.6 Glossary

Cluster: A group of nodes that run and manage containerized applications.

Pod: The smallest deployable unit in Kubernetes, comprising one or more containers.

Service: An abstraction to expose and connect Pods within or outside the cluster.

Deployment: Manages updates and scaling for applications declaratively.

Ingress: Manages external HTTP/HTTPS access to services within the cluster.

Kubectl: A command-line tool for interacting with Kubernetes clusters.

Exercise

Exercise 1 - Choose the correct answer from the given options.

1. What is Kubernetes primarily used for?
a) Database Management
b) Container Orchestration
c) Application Deployment in IoT
d) Data Warehousing

2. Which of the following best describes Kubernetes?
a) A programming language for containerised applications
b) An operating system for servers
c) An open-source platform for managing containerised workloads and services
d) A cloud provider for hosting applications

Exercise 2 - Check if the sentence is true or false.

1. Kubernetes is a container orchestration platform that automates the deployment, scaling, and management of containerised applications.

2. Kubernetes is only used for managing virtual machines, not containers.

Exercise 3 - Answer the following questions in your own words.

1. What is the primary technology discussed in the introduction?

2. Which section explains the benefits of Kubernetes?

Exercise 4 - Fill the blank space with the correct word.

1. Kubernetes is an open-source platform designed for automating ________, scaling, and operations of application containers.

2. The primary purpose of Kubernetes is to manage ________ environments effectively.

Exercise 5 - Match each word or phrase in Column A with Column B

1. Overview of Kubernetes
2. Why Kubernetes?
3. Key Concepts and Terminologies
4. Kubernetes Alternatives
5. Kubernetes Features

a) Manages deployment, scaling, and operations of apps
b) A powerful container orchestration platform
c) Auto-scaling, Self-healing, Service discovery, Rolling updates
d) Docker Swarm, Apache Mesos, HashiCorp Nomad, Rancher
e) Pods, Nodes, Clusters, Namespaces, Services

Exercise 6 - The following questions consist of two statements: Assertion (A) and Reason (R). Answer these questions, selecting the appropriate options given below:

1. Assertion (A): Kubernetes enables the automation of container deployment, scaling, and management. **Reason (R):** Kubernetes functions as a hypervisor for virtual machines, ensuring complete isolation of resources.

Alternatives:

a) Assertion (A) is true, and Reason (R) is the correct reason for Assertion (A).
b) Assertion (A) is true, but Reason (R) is not the correct reason for Assertion (A).
c) Assertion (A) is false, but Reason (R) is true.
d) Assertion (A) is true, but Reason (R) is false.

s

2. Assertion (A): Kubernetes is designed to work with containerised applications in distributed systems. **Reason (R):** Kubernetes eliminates the need for cloud infrastructure by replacing it with standalone systems.

Alternatives:

a) Assertion (A) is true, and Reason (R) is the correct reason for Assertion (A).
b) Assertion (A) is true, but Reason (R) is not the correct reason for Assertion (A).
c) Assertion (A) is false, but Reason (R) is true.
d) Assertion (A) is true, but Reason (R) is false.

Exercise 7 - Answer the following questions in 50 - 80 words.

1. What is Kubernetes, and what is its primary purpose?
2. Name two key features that make Kubernetes a popular choice for container orchestration.

Exercise 8 - Answer the following questions in 100 - 120 words.

1. What is Kubernetes, and how does it work to orchestrate containerised applications?
2. Why has Kubernetes become the leading platform for managing containerised applications in modern software environments?

Answer

Exercise 1 - 1 b), 2 c).
Exercise 2 - 1 True, 2 False.
Exercise 3 - 1 Kubernetes, 2 Why.
Exercise 4 - 1 Deployment, 2 Containerised.

Exercise 5 – 1 b), 2 a), 3 e), 4 d), 5 c).
Exercise 6 - 1 d), 2 d).

Online Resources

Online Exam Paper: https://forms.gle/FgQsc4dmokcFucwM7

QR Code:

Online Video Link: https://www.youtube.com/playlist?list=PLzlh_31VWEFol5mWCIbjfeCm6Uj5vytnF

QR Code:

Chapter 2 - Setting up Kubernetes

Learning Objectives

Learn how to install Kubernetes on various platforms and set up a functional cluster.

Deploy your first application to a Kubernetes cluster and understand its basic components.

Understand the benefits and considerations of using a managed Kubernetes provider.

Set up and configure a local Kubernetes cluster for development and testing purposes.

2.1 Installation of Kubernetes

Installing Kubernetes requires careful planning and execution to ensure a smooth and functional setup. Kubernetes can be installed on various platforms, including on-premise systems, cloud environments, and even local development machines. Here's a step-by-step breakdown:

Prerequisites:

Before installing Kubernetes, ensure the following:

A compatible operating system such as Linux (Ubuntu, CentOS, or Debian) or Windows.

A minimum of 2 CPUs and 2GB of RAM per node for a basic cluster setup.

Proper network configuration and connectivity between nodes.

Administrative privileges on the systems.

Installation of necessary tools such as kubectl, Docker, and container runtime interface (CRI) compatible tools.

Setting Up the Environment:

Kubernetes requires at least two machines: one for the control plane and one or more for worker nodes. Virtual machines can also be used for this purpose. Make sure the system's hostname, IP address, and networking settings are correctly configured. Disable swap memory to ensure proper Kubernetes operation using the command swapoff -a and updating the fstab file.

Installing kubeadm, kubelet, and kubectl:

The kubeadm tool simplifies the installation process, while kubelet runs and manages workloads on cluster nodes. Install these components by following these steps:

Add the Kubernetes repository to your package manager:

```
curl -s https://packages.cloud.google.com/apt/doc/apt-key.gpg | sudo apt-key add -
echo "deb https://apt.kubernetes.io/ kubernetes-xenial main" | sudo tee
/etc/apt/sources.list.d/kubernetes.list
sudo apt-get update
```

Install the packages:

```
sudo apt-get install -y kubeadm kubelet kubectl
```

Hold the versions to prevent automatic updates:

```
sudo apt-mark hold kubeadm kubelet kubectl
```

Initializing the Control Plane:

Run the kubeadm init command on the control plane node to initialize the cluster:

```
sudo kubeadm init --pod-network-cidr=192.168.0.0/16
```

This will output instructions to set up kubectl for cluster management. Execute the suggested commands to configure kubectl:

```
mkdir -p $HOME/.kube
sudo cp -i /etc/kubernetes/admin.conf $HOME/.kube/config
sudo chown $(id -u):$(id -g) $HOME/.kube/config
```

Installing a Pod Network:

A pod network allows Kubernetes pods to communicate. Choose a compatible network plugin such as Calico, Flannel, or Weave Net. For example, to install Calico:

```
kubectl apply -f https://docs.projectcalico.org/manifests/calico.yaml
```

Joining Worker Nodes:

On each worker node, use the join command provided during the control plane initialization. If the command is lost, generate a new token on the control plane node:

```
kubeadm token create --print-join-command
```

Run the join command on each worker node to connect it to the cluster.

Verifying the Cluster:

Check the status of nodes and pods using the following commands:

```
kubectl get nodes
kubectl get pods --all-namespaces
```

All nodes should show a "Ready" status, indicating successful setup.

Optional: Deploy a Dashboard:

For cluster monitoring, deploy the Kubernetes Dashboard:

```
kubectl apply -f https://raw.githubusercontent.com/kubernetes/dashboard/v2.6.0/aio/deploy/recommended.yaml
```

Access the dashboard by creating a token and starting a proxy server:

```
kubectl proxy
```

Navigate to **http://localhost:8001/api/v1/namespaces/Kubernetes-dashboard/services/https:kubernetes-dashboard:/proxy/** in your browser.

With these steps, your Kubernetes cluster is ready for deploying containerized applications. The modular approach of Kubernetes ensures flexibility, scalability, and ease of management for modern applications.

2.2 Deploying your first application

After setting up a Kubernetes cluster, the next step is to deploy your first application. Kubernetes uses YAML configuration files to define and manage application deployments. Here's how to deploy a simple application:

Creating a Deployment:

A Deployment is a Kubernetes object that manages the lifecycle of pods. Create a YAML file for the Deployment, specifying details such as the container image and the number of replicas. For example, to deploy an Nginx web server, create a file named **nginx-deployment.yaml:**

```
apiVersion: apps/v1
kind: Deployment
metadata:
  name: nginx-deployment
spec:
  replicas: 2
  selector:
    matchLabels:
      app: nginx
  template:
    metadata:
      labels:
        app: nginx
    spec:
      containers:
      - name: nginx
        image: nginx:latest
        ports:
        - containerPort: 80
```

Apply the Deployment using the kubectl apply command:

```
kubectl apply -f nginx-deployment.yaml
```

Exposing the Application:

To make the application accessible, create a Service that exposes it. For instance, to expose the Nginx Deployment, use the following command:

```
kubectl expose deployment nginx-deployment --type=NodePort --port=80
```

This will create a Service with a **NodePort,** making the application accessible via **<NodeIP>:<NodePort>**.

Verifying the Deployment:

Check the status of the Deployment and the pods using:

```
kubectl get deployments
kubectl get pods
kubectl get services
```

Ensure that the pods are running, and the Service has been assigned a NodePort.

Accessing the Application:

Retrieve the NodePort assigned to the Service using:

```
kubectl describe service nginx-deployment
```

Access the application in a web browser or using **curl** at **http://<NodeIP>:<NodePort>.**

Scaling the Deployment:

Kubernetes allows you to scale applications easily. For example, to increase the replicas of the Nginx Deployment to 4, run:

```
kubectl scale deployment nginx-deployment --replicas=4
```

Verify the change:

```
kubectl get pods
```

Updating the Application:

To update the container image used by the Deployment, run:

```
kubectl set image deployment/nginx-deployment nginx=nginx:1.21
```

This triggers a rolling update, ensuring minimal downtime.

By following these steps, you have successfully deployed your first application on Kubernetes. The power of Kubernetes lies in its ability to automate and manage deployments, scaling, and updates with ease.

2.3 Choosing a Managed Provider

Choosing a managed Kubernetes provider can significantly simplify cluster management, enabling teams to focus on application development instead of infrastructure maintenance. Several managed Kubernetes services are available, each offering unique features and benefits. Here are key considerations and popular providers to help make an informed choice:

Key Considerations:

Ease of Setup: Managed providers often offer a user-friendly interface and predefined configurations to set up clusters quickly.

Scalability: Ensure the provider supports horizontal and vertical scaling to handle workload growth seamlessly.

Cost: Evaluate pricing models, including pay-as-you-go or reserved capacity, to align with your budget.

Integration: Check for integrations with other cloud services, such as databases, monitoring, and CI/CD tools.

Security: Look for features like role-based access control (RBAC), encryption, and compliance with industry standards.

Support: Managed providers often include technical support and SLA-backed uptime guarantees, which are critical for production environments.

Popular Managed Kubernetes Providers:

Google Kubernetes Engine (GKE): GKE, offered by Google Cloud, is one of the most robust managed Kubernetes solutions. It provides automatic upgrades, strong integration with Google Cloud services, and advanced networking options.

Amazon Elastic Kubernetes Service (EKS): EKS by AWS is known for its reliability and flexibility. It integrates seamlessly with other AWS services and offers features like managed node groups and Fargate for serverless Kubernetes.

Azure Kubernetes Service (AKS): AKS, from Microsoft Azure, is widely used for its ease of integration with Azure DevOps and native support for Windows containers.

IBM Kubernetes Service: IBM's offering is tailored for hybrid cloud environments, emphasising security and compliance.

DigitalOcean Kubernetes: DigitalOcean's Kubernetes platform is beginner-friendly, offering a simplified interface and cost-effective pricing.

Red Hat OpenShift: OpenShift is a Kubernetes-based platform emphasising developer productivity and enterprise-grade security, suitable for both on-premise and cloud environments.

Recommendations:

Services like DigitalOcean Kubernetes or GKE are excellent choices for small—to medium-sized projects due to their simplicity and cost-effectiveness. For enterprises, EKS, AKS, or OpenShift provide robust features and better support for scaling and compliance.

Additional Features to Look For:

Many managed providers offer value-added features such as auto-scaling, monitoring tools, and multi-cluster support. Assess these features based on your project's specific needs.

By choosing the right managed provider, you can offload operational complexities and focus on building and deploying applications efficiently.

2.4 Installing a Local Cluster

Setting up a local Kubernetes cluster is a crucial step for developers and administrators looking to test, develop, or familiarise themselves with Kubernetes in a controlled environment. A local cluster allows you to emulate the behaviour of a full-fledged Kubernetes setup without requiring extensive infrastructure or cloud services. Several tools are available to simplify the process, such as Minikube, Kind (Kubernetes in Docker), and MicroK8s. Here, we will outline the steps for installing a local cluster using Minikube, one of the most popular tools.

Prerequisites

Before installing Minikube, ensure your system meets the following requirements:

Operating System: Linux, macOS, or Windows.

Virtualization Support: Minikube requires a hypervisor like VirtualBox, Hyper-V, or Docker.

System Resources: At least 2 CPUs, 2GB of free memory, and 20GB of disk space.

Command-Line Tools: Install kubectl and a package manager like brew (for macOS) or choco (for Windows).

Installing Minikube

Download Minikube: Visit the Minikube releases page and download the appropriate version for your operating system. Alternatively, use a package manager like brew install minikube or choco install minikube.

Install Minikube: Follow the installation instructions specific to your operating system. Ensure the Minikube executable is added to your system's PATH for easier access.

Verify Installation: Run minikube version in your terminal to confirm successful installation.

Starting Your Cluster
To create a local Kubernetes cluster:
Open a terminal and run the command:

```
minikube start
```

This command initialises a single-node Kubernetes cluster locally. You can specify options like the driver (e.g., **--driver=docker** for Docker) and resource allocation.

Verify the cluster status using:

```
minikube status
```

Ensure all components (e.g., API server, scheduler, and controller manager) are running.

Accessing Your Cluster
Once the cluster is running:
Use **kubectl** to interact with the cluster. For example:

```
kubectl get nodes
```

This command lists all nodes in the cluster.

Minikube also provides a built-in dashboard for managing Kubernetes resources. Launch it using:

```
minikube dashboard
```

This opens a web-based interface for easier cluster management.

Configuring Add-Ons
Minikube supports various add-ons to enhance functionality, such as metrics-server, ingress, and DNS. Enable an add-on with:

```
minikube addons enable <addon-name>
```

For example, to enable the metrics-server for resource monitoring:

```
minikube addons enable metrics-server
```

Stopping and Deleting the Cluster
To stop the cluster, run:

```
minikube stop
```

This halts the cluster but preserves its state. To completely delete the cluster:

```
minikube delete
```

This removes all cluster resources and configurations.
By following these steps, you can set up a local Kubernetes cluster to experiment with workloads, troubleshoot configurations, or gain hands-on experience with Kubernetes. As you advance, you might explore other tools like Kind or MicroK8s for specific use cases or features.

2.5 Summary

Install Kubernetes tools (kubeadm, kubelet, kubectl) on a supported OS with at least 2 CPUs and 2GB RAM.
Disable swap and configure networking; initialize the control plane with kubeadm init.
Set up a pod network (e.g., Calico) and join worker nodes using kubeadm join.
Deploy applications with a YAML file and expose them using NodePort.
Choose a managed provider based on ease of setup, scalability, and cost.
For local clusters, use Minikube for a single-node setup and manage with kubectl.

2.6 Glossary

Control Plane: Manages the Kubernetes cluster, including API server and scheduler.

Worker Node: Cluster machines that run containerized applications.

kubectl: Command-line tool for managing Kubernetes clusters.

Pod: The smallest deployable unit in Kubernetes containing containers.

Deployment: Manages the lifecycle and scaling of pods in Kubernetes.

Service: Exposes pods for network access, enabling communication and traffic routing.

Exercise

Exercise 1 - Choose the correct answer from the given options.

1. Which of the following is the first step in setting up Kubernetes?
a) Deploying a container
b) Installing Kubernetes
c) Creating a pod
d) Setting up cloud storage

2. Which of these is NOT a common method for installing Kubernetes?
a) kubeadm
b) Minikube
c) Docker Compose
d) Helm

Exercise 2 - Check if the sentence is true or false.

1. Kubernetes can be installed manually or by using a package manager like kubectl.
2. The first step in setting up Kubernetes is to deploy your first application.

Exercise 3 - Answer the following questions in your own words.

1. What is the primary focus when setting up Kubernetes?
2. Which section focuses on how to install Kubernetes?

Exercise 4 - Fill the blank space with the correct word.

1. Kubernetes is an open-source platform designed for automating ________, scaling, and operations of application containers.
2. The primary purpose of Kubernetes is to manage ________ environments effectively.

Exercise 5 - Match each word or phrase in Column A with Column B

1. Installation of Kubernetes

2. Deploying your first application
3. Choosing a Managed Provider
4. Installing a Local Cluster
5. Configuring Kubernetes Components

a) GKE, AKS, EKS, DigitalOcean Kubernetes, OpenShift
b) Creating Pods, Services, and Deployments
c) Minikube, Kind, MicroK8s, K3s, Rancher Desktop
d) Setting up API server, Controller Manager, and Scheduler
e) Installing kubeadm, kubectl, and kubelet

Exercise 6 - The following questions consist of two statements: Assertion (A) and Reason (R). Answer these questions, selecting the appropriate options given below:

1. Assertion (A): Installing Kubernetes requires setting up multiple components, including a master node and worker nodes.
Reason (R): Kubernetes only requires a single-node setup for production environments, which simplifies installation.
Alternatives:
a) Assertion (A) is true, and Reason (R) is the correct reason for Assertion (A).
b) Assertion (A) is true, but Reason (R) is not the correct reason for Assertion (A).
c) Assertion (A) is false, but Reason (R) is true.
d) Assertion (A) is true, but Reason (R) is false.

2. Assertion (A): Choosing a managed Kubernetes provider can save time by handling infrastructure and maintenance tasks.
Reason (R): Managed providers allow full customisation of Kubernetes clusters, including hardware configurations.
Alternatives:
a) Assertion (A) is true, and Reason (R) is the correct reason for Assertion (A).
b) Assertion (A) is true, but Reason (R) is not the correct reason for Assertion (A).
c) Assertion (A) is false, but Reason (R) is true.
d) Assertion (A) is true, but Reason (R) is false.

Exercise 7 - Answer the following questions in 50 - 80 words.
1. What are the general steps involved in installing Kubernetes?
2. What tools can be used to install Kubernetes on a local machine?

Exercise 8 - Answer the following questions in 100 - 120 words.
1. What are the different methods to install Kubernetes, and what factors should be considered when choosing an installation method?
2. Describe the step-by-step process of installing Kubernetes on a cloud provider or local machine. What tools are commonly used in the installation process?

Answer

Exercise 1 - 1 b), 2 c).
Exercise 2 - 1 True, 2 False.

Exercise 3 - 1 Setup, 2 Installation.
Exercise 4 - 1 Deployment, 2 Containerised.
Exercise 5 - 1 e), 2 b), 3 a), 4 c), 5 d).
Exercise 6 - 1 b), 2 b).

Online Resources

Online Exam Paper: https://forms.gle/XTJhgzVA4MrDCEgG8

QR Code:

Chapter 3 - Running Applications

Learning Objectives

Understand the concept of Pods and how they are used to run containers in Kubernetes.
Learn about ReplicaSets and their role in ensuring application availability and scaling.
Gain knowledge of Deployments for managing the lifecycle of applications and updates.
Understand the use of StatefulSets for managing stateful applications with persistent storage.
Learn how to create and manage Jobs for running batch or one-time tasks in Kubernetes.

3.1 Pods

In Kubernetes, a Pod is the smallest and most basic deployable unit that can be created and managed. A Pod represents a single instance of a running process in a cluster and encapsulates one or more containers, such as Docker containers. While a Pod typically runs a single container, it is designed to support multiple containers that need to operate in tight coupling. The containers in a Pod share the same network namespace, which means they can communicate with each other using localhost and share storage volumes. This feature allows applications that require multiple containers to run together, like a main application container and a helper container, within a single Pod.

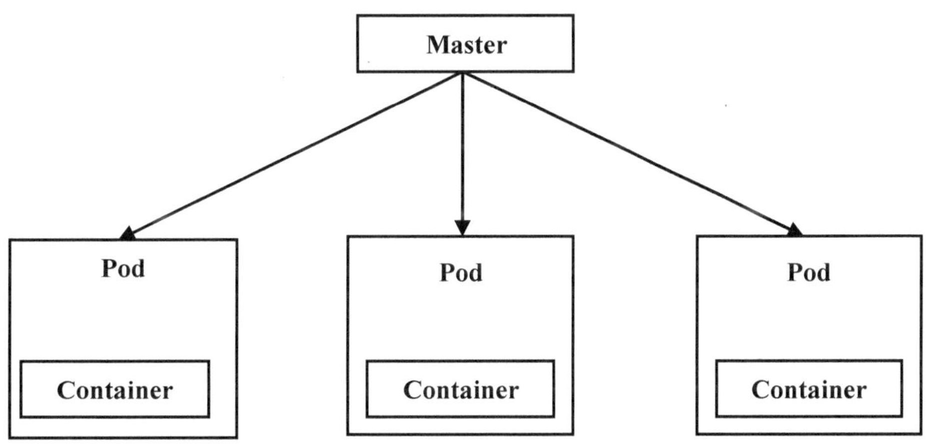

Each Pod is ephemeral and is intended to live for a short duration. They can be automatically managed and scaled by Kubernetes, but their lifecycle is tied to the workload (such as a Deployment or StatefulSet) that created them. Pods are scheduled to run on nodes in the Kubernetes cluster, with Kubernetes ensuring that the application is always running as per the desired configuration. If a Pod fails or gets terminated, Kubernetes will automatically create a new Pod to replace it, ensuring high availability and scalability of applications.

Pods can be configured with various specifications like resource requests and limits (CPU, memory), environmental variables, and volumes, making them adaptable to different application requirements. The ability to mount persistent volumes enables Pods to maintain state across restarts. While Pods are essential building blocks of Kubernetes, they are often managed indirectly through higher-level abstractions like Deployments, ReplicaSets, and StatefulSets, which handle tasks such as scaling, rolling updates, and management of Pod replicas.

In a production environment, the use of Pods is crucial for microservices-based architectures, where different components of an application can be encapsulated into separate containers within the same Pod. This allows Kubernetes to manage and scale complex applications effectively. Pods also help streamline application deployments by reducing operational complexity and ensuring consistency in how containers are deployed across the cluster.

3.2 ReplicaSets

A ReplicaSet is a key component in Kubernetes that ensures a specified number of identical Pods are running at any given time. The primary role of a ReplicaSet is to maintain the desired state of the application by ensuring that the correct number of Pod replicas are running across the cluster. If a Pod fails or gets deleted, the ReplicaSet will automatically create a new Pod to replace it, ensuring that the desired number of Pods is always maintained.
ReplicaSets are particularly important for providing high availability and scalability to applications. They allow Kubernetes to maintain a consistent number of Pods running in a cluster, even in the face of node failures or maintenance activities. For instance, if one node goes down, the ReplicaSet will ensure that the desired number of Pods are rescheduled on other available nodes, thereby ensuring the application's resilience and reliability.

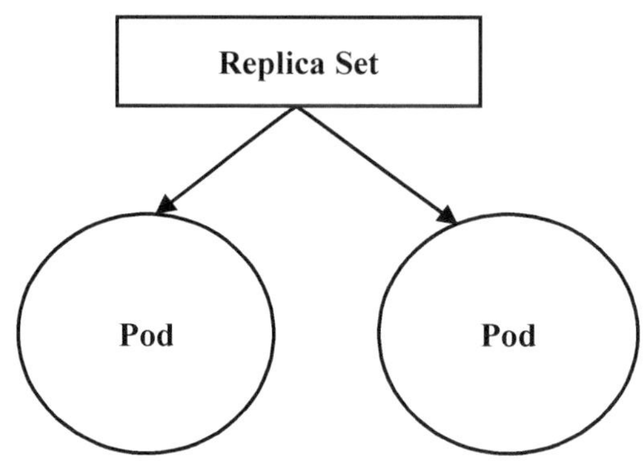

A ReplicaSet is defined by a set of specifications, such as the number of replicas (Pod instances) to maintain, the label selector used to identify the Pods it manages, and the template that defines the Pods' configuration. The label selector ensures that only Pods matching certain criteria are included in the ReplicaSet's management, allowing for precise control over which Pods are handled. The Pod template, on the other hand, contains the configuration for the Pods, such as container images, environment variables, ports, and resource limits.
One of the significant benefits of ReplicaSets is that they enable seamless scaling of applications. By adjusting the number of replicas, users can easily scale the application up or down depending on the traffic or resource requirements. For example, increasing the number of replicas allows the application to handle more requests, while decreasing it saves resources during low-traffic periods. This dynamic scaling ensures optimal resource usage and performance.
While ReplicaSets are crucial for ensuring that a given number of Pods are always running, they are typically managed indirectly through higher-level Kubernetes objects such as Deployments. Deployments provide an abstraction over ReplicaSets by adding features like rolling updates, versioned deployments, and rollback capabilities. Although a user can directly create and manage ReplicaSets, in most cases, Deployments are preferred because they simplify application management and provide additional functionality for handling updates.
Overall, ReplicaSets are essential for maintaining the stability, availability, and scalability of applications in a Kubernetes environment, ensuring that the application is always running with the right number of Pods to meet demand.

3.3 Deployments

A Deployment in Kubernetes is a higher-level abstraction that manages the lifecycle of Pods and ReplicaSets, simplifying the process of deploying and scaling applications. Deployments provide a declarative approach to application management, enabling users to define the desired state of the application and letting Kubernetes automatically manage the deployment process. This includes the creation, scaling, and rolling updates of Pods and ReplicaSets based on the defined configuration.

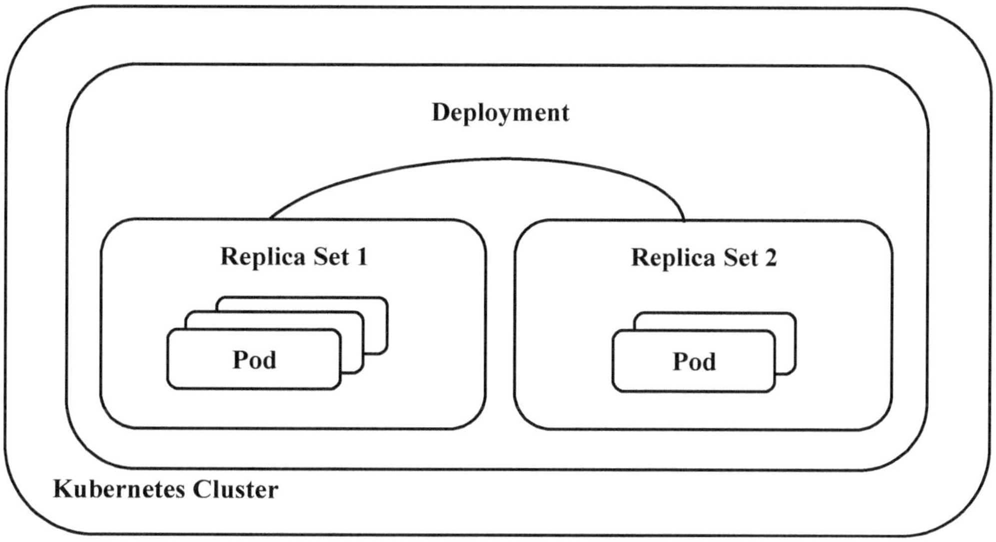

The primary function of a Deployment is to ensure that a specific number of replicas of a Pod are running at any given time. It automatically handles the creation and management of ReplicaSets, which, in turn, manage the individual Pods. With a Deployment, users can easily define how many Pod replicas should be running, the container images to use, and various configurations such as resource limits, environment variables, and volumes. This allows for consistent and reliable application deployment in a cluster.

Deployments offer several key features that enhance application management. One of the most significant features is rolling updates. When the application configuration or the container image needs to be updated, the Deployment can perform a rolling update, gradually replacing old Pods with new ones. This ensures minimal downtime and allows for a smooth transition between application versions. If an issue arises during the update, Kubernetes can automatically roll back the changes to the previous stable version, providing high availability and fault tolerance. Another important feature is versioned deployments, which allow tracking and managing different application versions. This enables Kubernetes to maintain and manage multiple versions of an application, making it easier to deploy new versions, roll back to previous ones, or perform canary releases where a small subset of users test the new version before it is fully rolled out.

Scaling applications is also simplified with Deployments. Users can adjust the number of Pod replicas easily by modifying the Deployment's configuration. Kubernetes will automatically scale the application by adding or removing Pods to match the desired replica count. This dynamic scaling allows applications to handle varying loads efficiently, ensuring that resources are used optimally while maintaining the desired level of availability.

Deployments also integrate well with Kubernetes services, allowing for load balancing and exposing the application to external traffic. As Pods are created or deleted during scaling or updates, the associated services will automatically route traffic to the available Pods, ensuring a consistent user experience without manual intervention.

Kubernetes Deployments provide a robust, automated, and scalable way to manage applications in a cluster. By leveraging features such as rolling updates, versioning, and automatic scaling, Deployments simplify the deployment process, reduce the risk of downtime, and ensure that applications remain available and resilient.

3.4 StatefulSets

A StatefulSet is a Kubernetes controller designed to manage the deployment and scaling of applications that require persistent state and stable, unique network identifiers. Unlike Deployments and ReplicaSets, which are suitable for stateless applications, StatefulSets are specifically tailored for applications that need to maintain their state across Pod restarts, ensuring that each instance (Pod) is uniquely identifiable and can be reliably persisted. StatefulSets provide a set of important guarantees that make them ideal for stateful applications such as databases, queues, or clustered services. The most notable feature is stable, unique network identities. Each Pod in a StatefulSet is assigned a unique, persistent name, which persists across restarts. This name is based on the StatefulSet name and an ordinal index (e.g., my-app-0, my-app-1, my-app-2). This stable identity allows Pods to communicate with each other using predictable DNS names, essential for clustered applications that require direct communication between instances.

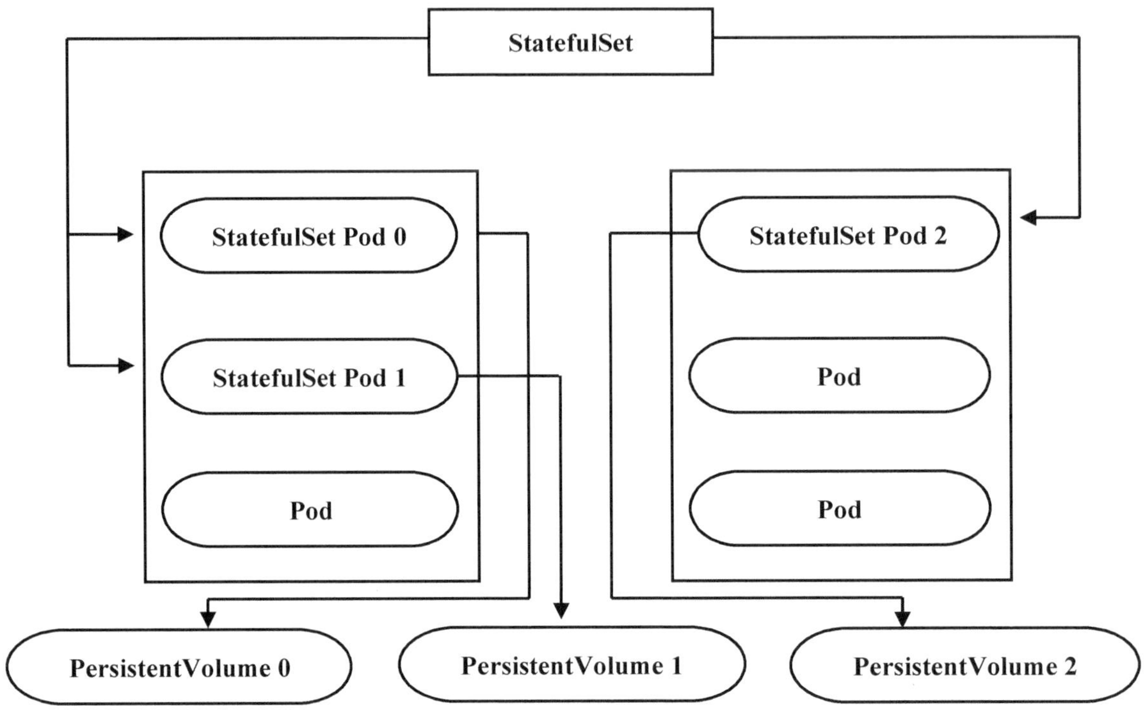

Another crucial feature of StatefulSets is persistent storage. StatefulSets are typically used in conjunction with PersistentVolumeClaims (PVCs), which are linked to storage volumes that persist even if the Pod is rescheduled or restarted. Each Pod in the StatefulSet can have its own PVC, which ensures that the application's data remains intact even if the Pod is destroyed and recreated. This makes StatefulSets ideal for applications that need to retain their data across restarts or scaling operations.

The StatefulSet controller ensures that the Pods are created, deleted, and updated in a specific order. Sequential scaling and rolling updates are key features of StatefulSets. When scaling up or down, StatefulSets will create or delete Pods one by one, ensuring that the application maintains its consistency and availability. During a rolling update, the controller will update Pods in a predictable order (from the highest index to the lowest) to minimise disruption and maintain the application's stateful behaviour.

StatefulSets also provides ordered, graceful deployment and termination of Pods. When a StatefulSet is deployed, the Pods are created in a specific order (e.g., my-app-0, my-app-1, my-app-2). Similarly, during termination, Pods are deleted in reverse order, ensuring that the application can handle the shutdown process gracefully, particularly when there is a dependency between Pods or a need for specific termination procedures.

One common use case for StatefulSets is for applications that rely on distributed storage systems or stateful services like databases (e.g., MySQL, PostgreSQL), message brokers (e.g., Kafka), or other clustered systems. These applications often require that each Pod maintain its own state and configuration, and StatefulSets ensure that the right amount of Pods is available in the correct order, with persistent storage and stable network identities.

While StatefulSets are a powerful tool for managing stateful applications, they come with some complexity compared to stateless workloads managed by Deployments. For example, managing stateful applications typically requires more careful planning around persistent storage and network configuration. However, for scenarios where persistence and stable identity are essential, StatefulSets are an indispensable feature in Kubernetes.

StatefulSets are a specialised resource in Kubernetes that enables the management of stateful applications. By ensuring stable network identities, persistent storage, and ordered Pod management, StatefulSets provide the necessary guarantees for applications that need to maintain state across restarts, scaling, and updates, making them a critical component for deploying complex, stateful services in a Kubernetes environment.

3.5 Jobs

A Job in Kubernetes is a controller used to manage the execution of batch or one-off tasks that run to completion. Unlike long-running applications that require continuous service, Jobs are designed for workloads that are finite in nature and must be completed once, such as data processing, backups, or batch computations. The main function of a Job is to ensure that a specified number of Pods successfully terminate, indicating the completion of the task. Once the job has finished, the Pods associated with it are terminated, freeing up resources.

Jobs are defined by specifying the desired number of completions, which represents the number of successful Pods that need to run and complete the task. The Job controller ensures that the specified number of Pods are created and executed. If a Pod fails, the Job controller will create a new Pod to replace it and ensure the overall job is completed successfully. Jobs also support parallel execution of Pods, allowing tasks to be distributed across multiple Pods, enhancing performance for workloads that can be divided into smaller, independent sub-tasks.

One important concept within Jobs is parallelism. When defining a Job, you can set the parallelism parameter, which controls how many Pods can run concurrently. This is especially useful when there is a need to process a large number of independent tasks in parallel. Jobs also allow you to specify the maximum number of Pods that should be retried if a failure occurs, through the backoffLimit parameter. This ensures that failed Pods do not retry indefinitely, which could otherwise lead to resource exhaustion.

Jobs can also be configured with completions to define how many successful Pods need to complete the task. For example, if a Job is set with completions: 5, the controller will ensure that five Pods successfully finish their execution before the Job is considered complete. This feature makes Jobs particularly well-suited for tasks that require a specific number of successful completions, such as processing a batch of records or performing multiple iterations of a task.

Another significant feature of Jobs is CronJobs. A CronJob allows you to schedule Jobs to run at specified times or intervals, similar to the way cron jobs work on Linux systems. This is useful for recurring tasks such as regular backups, log rotations, or batch data processing, enabling automated execution without requiring manual intervention.

Jobs provide important features for ensuring task completion in Kubernetes, such as retry logic, parallel execution, and scheduling. These features are crucial when dealing with tasks that are not intended to run continuously but must be executed reliably and accurately. Kubernetes will ensure that the desired number of Pods are completed, even in the face of failure or resource issues, making Jobs ideal for a wide range of batch processing and one-time execution tasks.

Kubernetes Jobs is a powerful tool for managing batch workloads that need to run to completion. Whether processing data, executing administrative tasks, or running periodic maintenance, Jobs ensures that tasks are completed successfully, with the flexibility to handle retries, parallelism, and scheduling. By utilising Jobs, organisations can automate and manage finite workloads in a Kubernetes cluster, ensuring reliability, scalability, and efficiency.

3.6 Summary

Pods: The smallest deployable unit in Kubernetes, usually containing one or more containers that share network and storage resources.
ReplicaSets: Ensures a specified number of identical Pods are running at all times, providing high availability and scalability.
Deployments: A higher-level abstraction for managing Pods and ReplicaSets, offering features like rolling updates and scaling.
StatefulSets: Used for applications that require persistent state, stable network identities, and ordered scaling, such as databases.
Jobs: Manages finite tasks that need to run to completion, with support for parallelism, retries, and scheduling through CronJobs.

3.7 Glossary

Pod: The smallest deployable unit in Kubernetes, typically running one or more containers in the same network namespace.
ReplicaSet: Ensures a desired number of Pod replicas are maintained for high availability and reliability.
Deployment: Manages the lifecycle of Pods and ReplicaSets, providing features like rolling updates, versioning, and scaling.
StatefulSet: Used for stateful applications that require persistent storage and stable network identities, ensuring ordered scaling and updates.
Job: A controller for managing finite tasks that run to completion, allowing for parallel execution and retry logic.

Exercise

Exercise 1 - Choose the correct answer from the given options.

1. What is the smallest and simplest Kubernetes object used to deploy an application?
a) Deployment
b) ReplicaSet
c) Pod
d) StatefulSet

2. Which of the following is NOT a characteristic of a Pod in Kubernetes?
a) It can contain multiple containers.
b) It is the basic scheduling unit in Kubernetes.
c) It ensures high availability by replicating itself automatically.
d) It shares network and storage resources among containers.

Exercise 2 - Check if the sentence is true or false.

1. A Pod in Kubernetes can contain one or more containers that share the same network namespace.
2. ReplicaSets ensure a specified number of pod replicas are running at any given time.

Exercise 3 - Answer the following questions in your own words.

1. What is the smallest deployable unit in Kubernetes?
2. What ensures the desired number of pod replicas are running?

Exercise 4 - Fill the blank space with the correct word.

1. A ________ is the smallest deployable unit in Kubernetes that can run one or more containers.
2. A Pod can host multiple ________ that share the same network and storage.

Exercise 5 - Match each word or phrase in Column A with Column B

1. Pods
2. ReplicaSets
3. Deployments
4. StatefulSets
5. Jobs

a) Manages updates to ReplicaSets
b) Ensures a specified number of pod replicas run
c) Runs tasks that terminate upon completion
d) Smallest deployable units in Kubernetes
e) Manages stateful applications with unique identities

Exercise 6 - The following questions consist of two statements: Assertion (A) and Reason (R). Answer these questions, selecting the appropriate options given below:

1. Assertion (A): Pods are the smallest deployable units in Kubernetes.
Reason (R): Pods in Kubernetes represent a collection of containers running on different physical machines.
Alternatives:
a) Assertion (A) is true, and Reason (R) is the correct reason for Assertion (A).
b) Assertion (A) is true, but Reason (R) is not the correct reason for Assertion (A).
c) Assertion (A) is false, but Reason (R) is true.
d) Assertion (A) is true, but Reason (R) is false.

2. Assertion (A): ReplicaSets ensure that a specified number of pod replicas are running at all times.
Reason (R): ReplicaSets automatically roll back to previous versions of an application when updates fail.
Alternatives:
a) Assertion (A) is true, and Reason (R) is the correct reason for Assertion (A).
b) Assertion (A) is true, but Reason (R) is not the correct reason for Assertion (A).
c) Assertion (A) is false, but Reason (R) is true.
d) Assertion (A) is true, but Reason (R) is false.

Exercise 7 - Answer the following questions in 50 - 80 words.

1. What is a Pod in Kubernetes, and what does it represent?
2. How does Kubernetes ensure high availability using ReplicaSets?

Exercise 8 - Answer the following questions in 100 - 120 words.

1. What is a Pod in Kubernetes, and why is it considered the smallest deployable unit? Discuss its structure and use cases.
2. Explain the role of ReplicaSets in Kubernetes. How do they ensure high availability and fault tolerance for applications?

Answer

Exercise 1 - 1 c), 2 c).
Exercise 2 - 1 True, 2 True.
Exercise 3 - 1 Pods, 2 ReplicaSets.
Exercise 4 - 1 Pod, 2 Containers.
Exercise 5 - 1 d), 2 b), 3 a), 4 e), 5 c).

Exercise 6 - 1 d), 2 b).

Online Resources

Online Exam Paper: https://forms.gle/sgfA5LJovZMaWktQA

QR Code:

Chapter 4 - Service and Networking

Learning Objectives

Understand how to configure external access to Kubernetes services for application communication.
Learn how load balancing works in Kubernetes to distribute traffic efficiently across Pods.
Explore Kubernetes networking concepts, including Pod-to-Pod communication and network policies.
Understand the different types of services in Kubernetes and their role in exposing applications.

4.1 External Access to Services

In modern cloud-native architectures, external access to services plays a crucial role in ensuring that applications and microservices are accessible to clients, users, or other external systems. This section delves into the various methods and strategies for managing external access to services within a cloud infrastructure.

External access can be achieved through different mechanisms depending on the requirements and the type of service being exposed. One of the most common methods is using load balancers. Load balancers act as intermediaries between the client and the services hosted in the backend. They distribute incoming traffic across multiple service instances to ensure high availability, performance, and fault tolerance. In cloud environments, services like Amazon Elastic Load Balancer (ELB) or Azure Load Balancer are typically used to handle external access to applications.

Another method for managing external access is the use of API Gateways. An API Gateway acts as a single entry point for all incoming API requests and routes them to the appropriate service. API Gateways are particularly useful in microservices architectures, where they can provide centralised authentication, authorisation, rate limiting, logging, and monitoring. Popular solutions like Kong, Nginx, or AWS API Gateway provide a way to expose multiple microservices to the outside world while maintaining security and performance.

Ingress controllers are also widely used to expose services in Kubernetes environments. Ingress is a set of rules that allow inbound connections to reach services in a Kubernetes cluster. The Ingress controller is responsible for managing these rules and directing traffic to the correct services. Ingress can be configured to handle various types of traffic, including HTTP, HTTPS, and TCP, making it a flexible solution for exposing services externally.

Security is a critical concern when providing external access to services. To ensure the protection of sensitive data and prevent unauthorised access, firewalls and virtual private networks (VPNs) are often used. Firewalls can control inbound and outbound traffic based on a set of security rules, allowing only authorised traffic to reach services. VPNs, on the other hand, provide a secure, encrypted connection between a client and the services, making it a suitable option for scenarios that require heightened security and privacy.

In some cases, services may need to be accessed from multiple regions or availability zones. Global load-balancing solutions can be used to ensure that traffic is intelligently routed to the nearest or most responsive data centre. This method ensures that users across different locations can access services with minimal latency and high availability.

Finally, monitoring and logging play an essential role in managing external access. Tools like Prometheus, Grafana, and ELK stack (Elasticsearch, Logstash, Kibana) can help in tracking the performance, security, and overall health of services exposed to external clients. This data is crucial for diagnosing issues, identifying potential vulnerabilities, and optimising access mechanisms.

Providing external access to services requires a combination of strategies, including load balancing, API gateways, ingress controllers, security protocols, and monitoring tools. By carefully choosing and implementing these solutions, organisations can ensure that their services are both accessible and secure for external users and clients.

4.2 Load Balancing

Load balancing is a fundamental concept in distributed systems that ensures the efficient distribution of network traffic across multiple servers or instances of a service. It is critical for maintaining high availability, scalability, and fault tolerance within modern cloud-native architectures. This section explores the principles of load balancing, its various strategies, and its impact on system performance and reliability.

At its core, load balancing is responsible for distributing incoming client requests across multiple backend services or servers to prevent any single resource from becoming overwhelmed. This process helps to optimize resource utilization, reduce response times, and prevent service outages. By spreading traffic across multiple servers, load balancing can handle increased traffic loads and ensure the system remains responsive even under peak conditions.

There are two main types of load balancing: hardware load balancing and software load balancing. Hardware load balancers are physical devices that distribute traffic among servers based on predefined algorithms. While hardware load balancers can offer high performance, they tend to be more expensive and less flexible compared to software-based solutions. On the other hand, software load balancers, often implemented in cloud environments, are typically more cost-effective and can be easily scaled or reconfigured as needed.

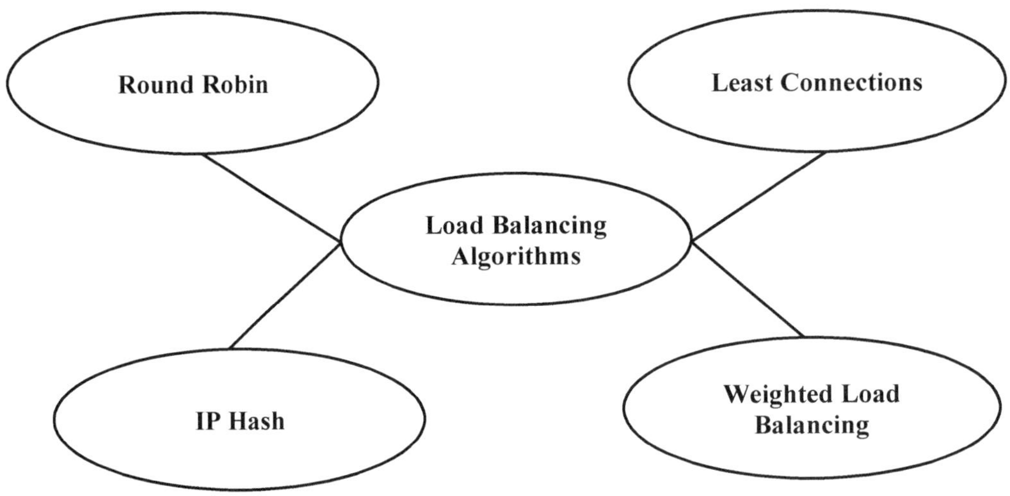

Load balancing algorithms determine how traffic is distributed among available servers. Some of the most common algorithms include:

Round Robin: This is one of the simplest load-balancing algorithms. It distributes client requests sequentially to each server in a cyclic manner. While it works well for services with similar load characteristics, it may not be suitable for applications with varying resource demands.

Least Connections: This algorithm routes traffic to the server with the fewest active connections, ensuring that no single server is overloaded. It is particularly useful for services with long-running connections or variable traffic loads.

IP Hash: In this method, a hash of the client's IP address is used to determine which server will handle the request. This can help maintain session persistence, where a client is always routed to the same server during its session.

Weighted Load Balancing: Servers can be assigned weights based on their performance or resource capacity. The load balancer distributes traffic according to these weights, allowing more powerful servers to handle a higher volume of traffic.

In cloud environments, load balancing is typically implemented using cloud-native load balancers such as Amazon Elastic Load Balancer (ELB), Google Cloud Load Balancing, and Azure Load Balancer. These services offer automatic scaling, integration with other cloud services, and seamless management of traffic distribution without requiring manual intervention. Cloud load balancers often provide advanced features such as SSL termination, HTTP/2 support, and health checks, ensuring both security and optimal performance.

For containerised applications, particularly those running on platforms like Kubernetes, ingress controllers and service meshes like Istio or Linkerd can be used for load balancing. Ingress controllers manage external traffic routing to services within a Kubernetes cluster, while service meshes handle inter-service communication within the cluster. These solutions allow for advanced traffic management features such as rate limiting, retries, and canary deployments.

Global load balancing is also a key consideration in today's distributed architectures. For organizations with a global user base, ensuring that traffic is routed to the nearest or most responsive data center is essential for minimizing latency and improving user experience. Global load balancers typically use a combination of geolocation-based routing, health checks, and traffic optimisation techniques to ensure users are directed to the best available server or data center.

One of the key benefits of load balancing is its ability to enhance fault tolerance. If a backend server fails, the load balancer automatically reroutes traffic to healthy servers, ensuring continued availability. This automatic failover mechanism is essential for maintaining service uptime and preventing disruption to end users.

Finally, it is important to monitor the performance of load-balancing systems. Tools like Prometheus, Grafana, and Datadog can be used to track key metrics such as response times, server health, and traffic distribution patterns. By continuously monitoring these metrics, organisations can proactively identify potential bottlenecks or performance issues and optimise the load-balancing configuration accordingly.

Load balancing is a critical component of scalable and resilient distributed systems. By effectively distributing traffic across multiple servers or instances, load balancing helps ensure high availability, optimised performance, and fault tolerance. With a variety of load-balancing algorithms, cloud-based solutions, and monitoring tools available, organisations can implement load-balancing strategies that meet the demands of their applications and users.

4.3 Networking & Pos-to-Pod Communication

Networking and pod-to-pod communication are fundamental aspects of modern cloud-native architectures, particularly in containerised environments like Kubernetes. As microservices architectures continue to grow in complexity, ensuring seamless communication between containers, or pods, becomes essential. This section explores the key principles of networking in cloud-native environments, focusing on pod-to-pod communication, its challenges, and the technologies that enable efficient networking within a Kubernetes cluster.

In Kubernetes, a pod is the smallest deployable unit, typically consisting of one or more containers that share the same network namespace, storage, and other resources. As applications grow, the number of pods and their need to communicate with each other increases, making pod-to-pod communication a crucial component of microservices-based systems. Kubernetes provides a flat networking model where each pod is assigned a unique IP address, allowing it to communicate with other pods in the cluster without requiring NAT (Network Address Translation). This flat networking model simplifies the complexity of managing communication between pods, enabling direct communication through IP addresses.

Pod-to-pod communication can be divided into two types: intra-cluster communication (within the same cluster) and inter-cluster communication (across different clusters). Intra-cluster communication is relatively straightforward, as Kubernetes ensures that every pod within the cluster can reach every other pod via their unique IP addresses. This is facilitated by the Kubernetes networking model, which mandates that all pods can communicate with each other by default, with no need for port mapping or complex network configurations.

For pod-to-pod communication to work effectively, Kubernetes uses various network plugins or Container Network Interfaces (CNIs) to implement the networking model. These CNIs, such as Calico, Flannel, Weave, and

Cilium, provide different approaches to network overlay, routing, and security. Each CNI comes with its own set of features and trade-offs, but all aim to provide reliable, scalable, and secure networking for Kubernetes pods. For instance, Calico is known for its high-performance network policies and scalability, while Weave simplifies network management and is easy to set up.

One of the challenges in pod-to-pod communication is ensuring network security. As pods communicate across various services, security mechanisms must be implemented to protect the data being transmitted. Kubernetes allows users to define Network Policies that control the traffic flow between pods. These policies can be used to specify which pods are allowed to communicate with each other, effectively limiting access to only trusted services and enhancing security within the cluster.

In addition to intra-cluster pod communication, inter-cluster communication becomes necessary when applications span multiple Kubernetes clusters. This can occur for several reasons, such as scaling across geographic regions or separating workloads for organizational purposes. Inter-cluster communication can be challenging because each cluster has its own network configuration, and Kubernetes do not natively support direct communication between pods across clusters. However, solutions like Istio (a service mesh) and Cilium (which extends Kubernetes networking) can help manage inter-cluster communication by providing advanced networking capabilities, including cross-cluster routing, service discovery, and consistent security policies across clusters.

To manage pod communication at scale, Kubernetes employs DNS-based service discovery. Kubernetes provides an internal DNS service, which allows pods to discover each other using domain names instead of IP addresses. When a service is created within Kubernetes, it is automatically assigned a DNS name, and all pods within the cluster can access that service by name. This eliminates the need to manage static IP addresses, making it easier to scale applications as pods are created or destroyed.

Another important aspect of pod-to-pod communication is traffic management, which ensures that requests between pods are routed efficiently and reliably. Kubernetes supports several mechanisms for managing traffic flow, such as Ingress Controllers for managing external traffic and Services for managing internal communication. A Service in Kubernetes is an abstraction that groups a set of pods and provides a stable IP address or DNS name to enable reliable communication. Services can be exposed internally or externally, and traffic can be load-balanced across the pods behind the service.

In scenarios where latency, high availability, and resiliency are critical, service meshes like Istio or Linkerd provide advanced traffic management capabilities. These tools offer features such as automatic retries, load balancing, circuit breaking, and service discovery, allowing for fine-grained control over how pod-to-pod communication occurs. Service meshes also enhance observability by providing metrics, tracing, and logging, helping operators monitor and optimise pod communication.

Networking and pod-to-pod communication are essential for the smooth functioning of containerised applications. Kubernetes and its associated network plugins provide a flexible, scalable networking model that ensures seamless communication between pods within a cluster. Organisations can secure, manage, and optimise pod-to-pod communication by leveraging network policies, DNS service discovery, and service meshes, ensuring high-performance and reliable communication between microservices in a distributed environment.

4.4 Summary

External Access: Methods like load balancers, API gateways, and ingress controllers ensure external connectivity to cloud services while maintaining security and performance.
Load Balancing: Distributes incoming traffic across multiple servers to ensure high availability, scalability, and fault tolerance.
API Gateways: Route API requests to the appropriate service and provide centralized management for authentication, rate limiting, and logging.
Pod-to-Pod Communication: Kubernetes enables seamless communication between containers within a cluster using unique IP addresses, facilitated by network plugins.
Security and Monitoring: Firewalls, VPNs, and monitoring tools (e.g., Prometheus, Grafana) ensure secure, optimised access and performance tracking for cloud-native services.

4.5 Glossary

Load Balancer: A tool that distributes traffic across multiple service instances to ensure availability and fault tolerance.
API Gateway: A centralized entry point for API requests that routes traffic to backend services.
Ingress Controller: A Kubernetes component that manages and routes inbound traffic to services within a cluster.
CNI (Container Network Interface): A set of plugins enabling network connectivity for pods in Kubernetes.
Service Mesh: Tools like Istio that manage microservices communication, offering features like load balancing, security, and observability.

Exercise

Exercise 1 - Choose the correct answer from the given options.

1. What is the primary purpose of a Service in Kubernetes?
a) To monitor container health
b) To provide stable networking and expose applications
c) To manage persistent volumes
d) To control container resource allocation

2. Which type of Kubernetes Service is used to expose applications to the internet?
a) ClusterIP
b) NodePort
c) LoadBalancer
d) Headless Service

Exercise 2 - Check if the sentence is true or false.

1. External access to Kubernetes services can be achieved through services like LoadBalancer, NodePort, or Ingress.
2. Kubernetes LoadBalancers automatically route traffic to the pods behind the service.

Exercise 3 - Answer the following questions in your own words.

1. What provides external access to services in Kubernetes?
2. What is used to distribute traffic across multiple pods?

Exercise 4 - Fill the blank space with the correct word.

1. In Kubernetes, ________ is used to expose services to external clients outside the cluster.
2. A ________ is a stable endpoint for accessing a service within a Kubernetes cluster, often used for load balancing.

Exercise 5 - Match each word or phrase in Column A with Column B

1. External Access to Services
2. Load Balancing
3. Networking & Pod-to-Pod Communication
4. Service Discovery
5. Ingress

a) Exposing services using NodePort, LoadBalancer, or Ingress
b) Distributing traffic across multiple pods evenly
c) Facilitates communication within the cluster using CNI plugins
d) DNS-based mechanism to locate services within a cluster
e) HTTP/HTTPS routing to distribute external traffic to services

Exercise 6 - The following questions consist of two statements: Assertion (A) and Reason (R). Answer these questions, selecting the appropriate options given below:

1. Assertion (A): External access to services in Kubernetes is typically achieved through LoadBalancer, NodePort, or Ingress controllers.

Reason (R): LoadBalancer services provide access to Kubernetes services from within the cluster only.

Alternatives:

a) Assertion (A) is true, and Reason (R) is the correct reason for Assertion (A).
b) Assertion (A) is true, but Reason (R) is not the correct reason for Assertion (A).
c) Assertion (A) is false, but Reason (R) is true.
d) Assertion (A) is true, but Reason (R) is false.

2. Assertion (A): Kubernetes services can use load balancing to distribute network traffic evenly among available pods.

Reason (R): Load balancing in Kubernetes automatically routes traffic only to pods that are in the 'Running' state.

Alternatives:

a) Assertion (A) is true, and Reason (R) is the correct reason for Assertion (A).
b) Assertion (A) is true, but Reason (R) is not the correct reason for Assertion (A).
c) Assertion (A) is false, but Reason (R) is true.
d) Assertion (A) is true, but Reason (R) is false.

Exercise 7 - Answer the following questions in 50 - 80 words.

1. What is the purpose of a Service in Kubernetes?

2. How can external traffic access services run inside a Kubernetes cluster?

Exercise 8 - Answer the following questions in 100 - 120 words.

1. What are the different ways to provide external access to services in Kubernetes, and how do you choose the right method based on your use case?

2. Explain the role of Kubernetes Services in enabling communication between Pods. How do they facilitate both internal and external access to applications?

Answer

Exercise 1 - 1 b), 2 c).
Exercise 2 - 1 True, 2 True.
Exercise 3 - 1 External Access, 2 Load Balancing.
Exercise 4 - 1 NodePort, 2 Service.
Exercise 5 - 1 a), 2 b), 3 c), 4 d), 5 e).
Exercise 6 - 1 b), 2 a).

Online Resources

Online Exam Paper: https://forms.gle/VK7U2FwcprCJJavy7

QR Code:

Chapter 5 - Configuration Management

Learning Objectives

Learn how to use ConfigMaps to inject configuration data into Kubernetes Pods.

Understand the best practices for managing configuration settings across multiple Pods using ConfigMaps.

Explore the use of Secrets in Kubernetes to securely store and manage sensitive data like passwords and API keys.

Gain knowledge on how to securely inject sensitive information into Pods using Kubernetes Secrets.

5.1 Injecting Pod Config with ConfigMaps

In Kubernetes, configuration management plays a critical role in managing complex deployments and ensuring consistency across environments. One of the core resources for configuration management in Kubernetes is ConfigMaps, which allow users to separate configuration from application code. This section will explore how to inject pod configurations using ConfigMaps.

A ConfigMap is a Kubernetes object that allows you to store non-sensitive data in the form of key-value pairs. These configurations can be injected into pods at runtime, ensuring that containers are able to access environment-specific settings without hardcoding values into the application code. By using ConfigMaps, you can decouple the configuration from the code, which makes it easier to manage and maintain.

To inject pod configurations with ConfigMaps, you typically define a ConfigMap resource and reference it within the pod specification. ConfigMaps can be used in several ways: environment variables, as volumes, or through command-line arguments passed to the container. By using environment variables, Kubernetes can automatically populate them with values from the ConfigMap, making them easily accessible to the application code. This method is commonly used for less complex configurations.

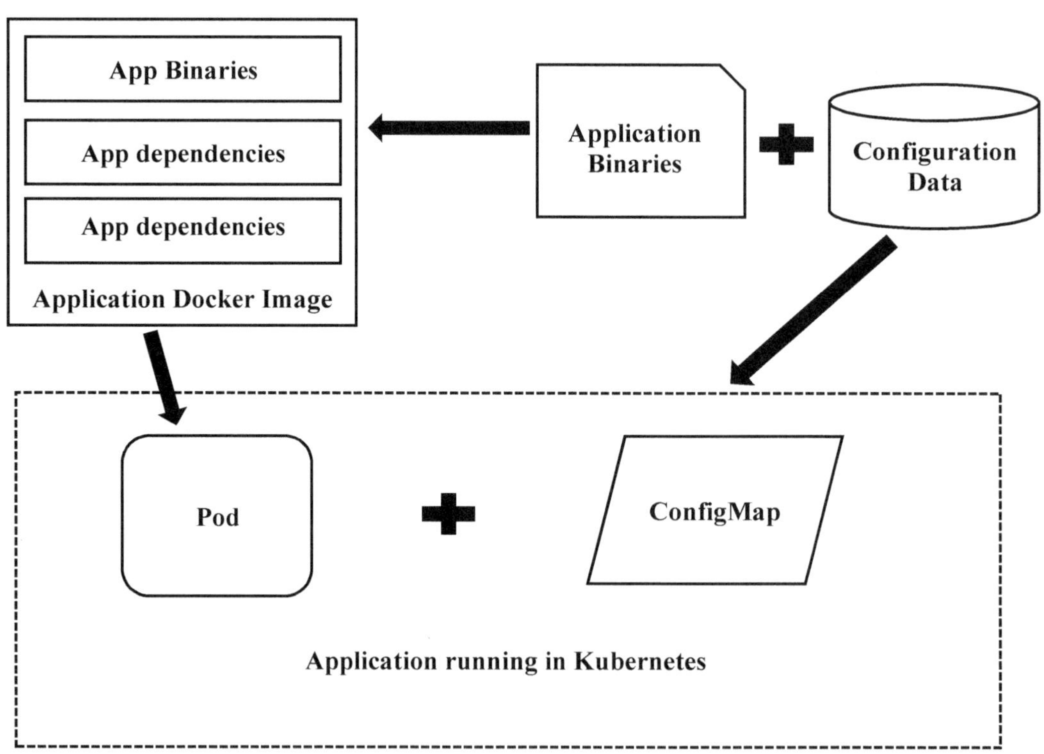

Another way to inject configurations is by mounting the ConfigMap as a volume. This allows files within the ConfigMap to be accessible as if they were files on the local filesystem of the pod. This method is useful when the application requires configuration files, such as JSON or YAML, instead of environment variables. By doing so, Kubernetes ensures that the configuration is updated automatically without requiring any code changes, enabling a smooth, continuous delivery workflow.

In practice, creating a ConfigMap is a straightforward process. You can either define it in YAML format and apply it with kubectl apply, or create it dynamically using the kubectl create configmap command. Once created, the ConfigMap can be used in a pod's specification under the envFrom or volumes section, depending on the intended injection method. Kubernetes will automatically populate the pod's environment or file system with the values defined in the ConfigMap.

One of the key advantages of using ConfigMaps for injecting configuration into pods is the ability to update configurations independently of the pod lifecycle. Suppose there is a need to modify the configuration. In that case, you can simply update the ConfigMap, and Kubernetes will automatically propagate the changes to the running pods without requiring a restart or manual intervention. However, it is important to note that this automatic update behaviour depends on how the ConfigMap is used in the pod. For example, when using volumes, updates to the ConfigMap are reflected on the filesystem automatically, but environment variables need the pod to be restarted to pick up the changes.

Injecting pod configurations with ConfigMaps is an effective way to manage application settings in Kubernetes. It provides flexibility, reduces the risk of misconfiguration, and ensures that your applications can adapt to different environments without changing the code. By using ConfigMaps, you not only maintain the separation of concerns but also enable better scalability and easier maintenance in Kubernetes clusters.

5.2 Using Secrets for Sensitive Data

In any application or infrastructure, managing sensitive data, such as passwords, API keys, or access tokens, is of paramount importance. Exposing sensitive information in an insecure way can lead to significant security vulnerabilities. In Kubernetes, sensitive data is typically managed using Secrets, a Kubernetes object designed specifically for storing and handling confidential information. This section explores how Kubernetes Secrets can be used to manage sensitive data securely within your cluster.

A Secret in Kubernetes is an object that stores sensitive information in the form of key-value pairs, much like a ConfigMap. However, unlike ConfigMaps, Secrets are designed with security in mind. When creating Secrets, Kubernetes provides the ability to store sensitive data in an encoded format, typically base64-encoded, to prevent it from being exposed in plain text within the cluster. While base64 encoding is not a robust encryption mechanism by itself, it serves as a basic layer of obfuscation and ensures that sensitive data is not immediately visible in logs or standard outputs.

Secrets can be injected into pods in several ways, making them flexible for a variety of use cases. The most common methods are injecting them as environment variables or mounting them as files within a pod. By using environment variables, sensitive data is made available to the application running in the pod, but is hidden from the user and logs unless explicitly requested. This method is suitable when the application needs to use sensitive data directly as part of its environment, such as accessing a database using a password or connecting to an external service with an API key.

Another approach for managing sensitive data with Secrets is to mount them as volumes. When mounted as a volume, the secret data becomes available as files within the pod's file system. This approach is often used when the application requires access to sensitive files, such as SSL certificates, private keys, or other configuration files that should not be exposed as environment variables. Mounting Secrets as volumes ensures that sensitive data is managed securely while remaining accessible to the application as needed.

While Kubernetes Secrets provide a convenient way to handle sensitive information, it is important to recognize that they come with certain limitations and security considerations. By default, Kubernetes stores Secrets in etcd, the distributed key-value store used by Kubernetes, in an unencrypted form. To enhance security, it is recommended to enable encryption at rest for etcd, ensuring that Secrets are encrypted while stored. Additionally, Kubernetes RBAC (Role-Based Access Control) policies should be used to control who has access to Secrets, ensuring that only authorized users and applications can retrieve or modify them.

Kubernetes also supports automatic rotation of Secrets, which can be valuable for keeping sensitive data fresh and secure. For example, you can periodically update a Secret to change credentials or tokens, and Kubernetes will automatically propagate the new value to any pods using the Secret. This feature helps reduce the risk of security breaches due to stale credentials or leaked secrets. However, to take full advantage of Secret rotation, your application should be designed to dynamically re-load secrets, either through Kubernetes mechanisms or through custom logic.

Using Secrets for sensitive data in Kubernetes offers a secure and manageable way to handle confidential information within your cluster. By leveraging Secrets, you can avoid storing sensitive data directly in code or environment variables, reducing the risk of accidental exposure. While Kubernetes provides mechanisms for securing and managing Secrets, it is important to follow best practices, such as enabling encryption at rest, using RBAC for access control, and periodically rotating sensitive information. By doing so, you ensure that your applications remain secure while complying with best practices in managing sensitive data.

5.3 Summary

ConfigMaps: Used in Kubernetes to store non-sensitive configuration data in key-value pairs, which can be injected into pods via environment variables or volumes.

Injecting Configs: ConfigMaps can be injected into pods through environment variables for simpler configurations or mounted as volumes for file-based configurations like JSON or YAML.

Secrets: Kubernetes provides a secure way to store sensitive data (e.g., passwords, API keys) in Secrets, which are base64-encoded and can be injected into pods as environment variables or mounted as files.

Secret Security: Secrets are stored in etcd and can be encrypted at rest for added security. Kubernetes RBAC controls access to Secrets.

Automatic Rotation: Kubernetes supports automatic rotation of Secrets to ensure sensitive data stays fresh and secure, with applications needing to handle dynamic reloading of updated Secrets.

5.4 Glossary

ConfigMap: A Kubernetes resource used to store non-sensitive configuration data in key-value pairs, which can be injected into pods.

Secret: A Kubernetes object designed to store sensitive data (e.g., passwords, tokens) securely using base64 encoding.

Environment Variables: Variables used to pass configuration data or sensitive information into a pod's containers.

Volume: A method in Kubernetes where a ConfigMap or Secret is mounted into a pod's filesystem to be accessed as files.

RBAC (Role-Based Access Control): A security mechanism in Kubernetes that controls access to resources like Secrets based on roles and permissions.

Exercise

Exercise 1 - Choose the correct answer from the given options.

1. What is the primary purpose of a ConfigMap in Kubernetes?
a) To store sensitive data
b) To manage persistent storage
c) To inject configuration data into Pods
d) To manage the scaling of applications

2. Which of the following can be stored in a ConfigMap?
a) Passwords
b) API keys
c) Non-sensitive configuration data like environment variables
d) Private keys

Exercise 2 - Check if the sentence is true or false.

1. ConfigMaps in Kubernetes allow you to inject non-sensitive configuration data into pods.

2. Secrets in Kubernetes are used to store non-sensitive data like configuration files and environment variables.

Exercise 3 - Answer the following questions in your own words.

1. What is used to inject configuration into pods?

2. What is used to manage sensitive data in Kubernetes?

Exercise 4 - Fill the blank space with the correct word.

1. ________ allows you to store non-sensitive configuration data that can be injected into pods as environment variables or mounted as files.

2. The ________ option in the pod specification allows you to inject configuration data into a pod using ConfigMap.

Exercise 5 - Match each word or phrase in Column A with Column B

1. Injecting Pod Config with ConfigMaps
2. Using Secrets for Sensitive Data
3. ConfigMap
4. Secret
5. Encryption in Secrets

a) Allows you to store and manage sensitive information.
b) Can store passwords, tokens, and other sensitive information.
c) Used for storing non-sensitive data like configuration files.
d) Provides an additional layer of security for sensitive data.
e) Stores environment variables, configuration files, and more.

Exercise 6 - The following questions consist of two statements: Assertion (A) and Reason (R). Answer these questions, selecting the appropriate options given below:

1. Assertion (A): ConfigMaps allow the injection of configuration data into Kubernetes Pods.
Reason (R): ConfigMaps are used exclusively for storing sensitive data, ensuring encrypted storage in Pods.

Alternatives:

a) Assertion (A) is true, and Reason (R) is the correct reason for Assertion (A).
b) Assertion (A) is true, but Reason (R) is not the correct reason for Assertion (A).
c) Assertion (A) is false, but Reason (R) is true.
d) Assertion (A) is true, but Reason (R) is false.

2. Assertion (A): Secrets in Kubernetes are used to store sensitive data, such as passwords and API keys.
Reason (R): Secrets are stored in plain text within the cluster, making them easily accessible to anyone with cluster access.
Alternatives:

a) Assertion (A) is true, and Reason (R) is the correct reason for Assertion (A).
b) Assertion (A) is true, but Reason (R) is not the correct reason for Assertion (A).
c) Assertion (A) is false, but Reason (R) is true.
d) Assertion (A) is true, but Reason (R) is false.

Exercise 7 - Answer the following questions in 50 - 80 words.

1. What is a ConfigMap in Kubernetes, and how is it used in configuration management?
2. How can you inject configuration data into a Pod using a ConfigMap?

Exercise 8 - Answer the following questions in 100 - 120 words.

1. What are ConfigMaps in Kubernetes, and how can they be used to inject configuration data into Pods? Explain the process in detail.
2. How do ConfigMaps help separate configuration data from application code in Kubernetes, and what are the advantages of this approach?

Answer

Exercise 1 - 1 c), 2 c).
Exercise 2 - 1 True, 2 False.
Exercise 3 - 1 ConfigMaps, 2 Secrets.
Exercise 4 - 1 ConfigMap, 2 env.
Exercise 5 - 1 c), 2 a), 3 e), 4 b), 5 d).
Exercise 6 - 1 b), 2 d).

Online Resources

Online Exam Paper: https://forms.gle/HU2G8bUSeiafuCT68

QR Code:

Chapter 6 - Resource Management

Learning Objectives

Understand how to set resource requests and limits for Pods to ensure optimal performance and prevent resource contention.

Learn how to assign resource quotas to namespaces to manage and control resource usage across multiple applications.

Explore best practices for monitoring resource usage in Kubernetes and identifying optimisation opportunities.

Gain knowledge of tools and strategies for analysing and optimising resource utilisation in a Kubernetes cluster.

Understand the impact of resource management on application stability, scalability, and cost efficiency.

6.1 Setting Resource Requests and Limits

In Kubernetes, efficient resource management is crucial for ensuring that applications run smoothly and efficiently on a cluster. One of the key aspects of resource management is setting resource requests and limits for containers, which can help ensure optimal allocation and prevent overuse of resources. This section focuses on understanding how to configure these settings effectively.

Resource Requests

A resource request is the amount of CPU and memory that a container needs to operate. Kubernetes uses resource requests to schedule pods on nodes that have enough resources available. When you define a resource request, Kubernetes ensures that the container is scheduled on a node that can accommodate the request. This guarantees that the container has the necessary resources to function properly.

The resource request is defined in the pod specification, under the resources field, and it includes both CPU and memory. For example, a container may request 500m CPU (which is half of a CPU core) and 256Mi of memory. If a pod doesn't specify resource requests, Kubernetes will assume the default value of zero for both CPU and memory. This can lead to resource contention, where the pod might not get enough resources to run efficiently.

Resource Limits

A resource limit defines the maximum amount of CPU and memory a container can consume. Setting resource limits helps prevent any single container from consuming all available resources on a node, which could negatively affect other containers running on the same node. If a container exceeds its resource limit, it might be throttled (for CPU) or killed and restarted (for memory), depending on the type of resource being exceeded.

Setting a resource limit ensures that containers do not consume excessive resources, which could impact the overall performance and stability of the cluster. By defining reasonable resource limits, you can avoid situations where a container consumes more than its fair share of CPU or memory, leading to poor performance or crashes in other containers.

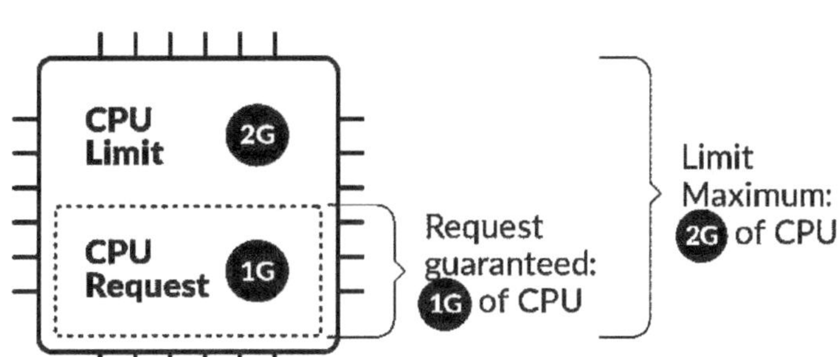

Request vs. Limit

While both resource requests and limits help manage resource allocation, they serve different purposes. The Kubernetes scheduler uses the resource request to place pods on nodes with enough available resources, whereas the resource limit is enforced at runtime to restrict the maximum usage of CPU and memory. It is important to set both request and limit values to ensure a balance between efficient scheduling and resource protection.

A common best practice is to set the resource request to a value that is sufficient for the container to function under typical conditions, while setting the limit to a slightly higher value to allow for occasional spikes in resource usage. This can help avoid both under-provisioning and over-provisioning of resources.

Tuning Resource Requests and Limits

Tuning the right values for requests and limits is crucial to achieve optimal performance. Setting these values too low could result in underutilisation of resources, while setting them too high can lead to inefficient use of cluster resources. It is essential to monitor application performance and resource usage regularly and adjust these values based on real-world data.

In some cases, Kubernetes provides an option to define requests and limits based on CPU and memory usage patterns over time. This allows for automatic adjustments to resource requests and limits as workload demands change. However, the most effective approach is to start with an estimated value, monitor usage, and iterate to refine resource settings.

Setting resource requests and limits is an essential practice for managing resources effectively in a Kubernetes environment. By specifying appropriate requests and limits for containers, you ensure that applications are allocated the right amount of resources for optimal performance. With careful tuning and monitoring, you can create a resource-efficient cluster that scales effectively and avoids resource contention.

6.2 Assigning Quotas to Namespaces

In a Kubernetes cluster, namespaces are used to organize resources and workloads into isolated environments. However, as multiple teams or applications share the same cluster, it's important to enforce resource usage constraints to ensure fair resource allocation and prevent a single team or application from consuming disproportionate resources. This is where ResourceQuotas come into play. Assigning quotas to namespaces helps manage and limit resource consumption within each namespace, ensuring that the cluster operates efficiently and fairly across all users and workloads.

Understanding ResourceQuotas

A ResourceQuota in Kubernetes is an object that provides constraints on the amount of resources a namespace can consume. These quotas can limit the total number of resources, such as CPU, memory, persistent volume claims, and the number of objects (e.g., Pods, Services, ConfigMaps) that can be created within a namespace. By setting ResourceQuotas, administrators can prevent one namespace from overconsuming resources at the expense of others.

The ResourceQuota is defined at the namespace level and can be applied to a specific set of resources, or even all resources, within the namespace. For example, an organisation might set a CPU limit for one team's namespace and a memory limit for another, ensuring that each team has a fair share of resources without disrupting other teams' workloads.

Configuring ResourceQuotas

To assign a ResourceQuota to a namespace, administrators need to define the quota specifications in a YAML file and apply it using kubectl. The specification includes the resource types (such as CPU, memory, and number of pods), along with the desired limits.

Here's an example of a simple ResourceQuota configuration in YAML format:

```
apiVersion: v1
kind: ResourceQuota
metadata:
  name: resource-quota-example
  namespace: my-namespace
spec:
  hard:
    cpu: "10"
    memory: 20Gi
    pods: "100"
```

In this example, the namespace my-namespace is limited to a maximum of 10 CPUs, 20Gi of memory, and 100 Pods. Once these limits are reached, any attempt to create additional resources beyond the defined quota will be rejected by Kubernetes.

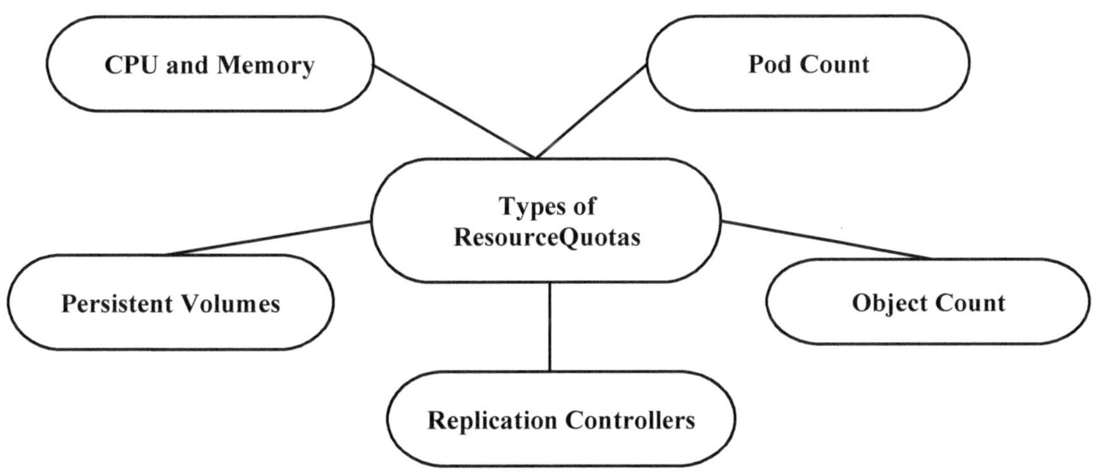

Types of ResourceQuotas

Resource Quotas in Kubernetes can manage various types of resources. Some of the common resource types include:

CPU and Memory: Limits on the total amount of CPU and memory that can be used across all resources within a namespace.

Pod Count: A limit on the total number of Pods that can be created in the namespace.

Persistent Volumes: A restriction on the number of persistent volume claims (PVCs) or the total storage capacity allocated in the namespace.

Object Count: Limits on the number of specific objects, such as Pods, Services, ConfigMaps, Secrets, and others, that can exist in the namespace.

Replication Controllers: A limit on the number of replication controllers (or Deployments, ReplicaSets) allowed within the namespace.

By carefully assigning quotas for these resource types, administrators can effectively control and optimise the resource usage for different teams or applications running in separate namespaces.

Benefits of Using ResourceQuotas

Assigning quotas to namespaces provides several key benefits:

Resource Isolation: By limiting the resources a namespace can consume, administrators ensure that one application or team cannot overwhelm the cluster by consuming excessive CPU, memory, or storage.

Fairness: Resource quotas enforce a fair distribution of resources across namespaces, preventing situations where one team's workloads consume all available resources, thus starving other teams or applications.

Cost Control: With resource quotas in place, organizations can control the cost of running multiple applications or environments in the same Kubernetes cluster. This is particularly important for organisations using cloud-based services where resource usage directly translates into cost.

Prevent Resource Exhaustion: Without resource quotas, the cluster might experience resource exhaustion, leading to performance degradation or application crashes. Resource quotas ensure that the cluster remains stable by preventing any namespace from consuming all the available resources.

Monitoring ResourceQuotas

Once quotas are in place, it's crucial to monitor their usage to ensure they're being respected and that no namespace is running into resource limits too frequently. Kubernetes provides tools such as Kubectl to describe resource quota to view the current usage of resources in a namespace and check how close it is to reaching the defined limits.

For example, to check the status of a ResourceQuota, you can run:

```
kubectl describe resourcequota resource-quota-example -n my-namespace
```

This command shows the current resource usage in the namespace, along with the limits and how much of each resource has been consumed. By regularly monitoring quotas, administrators can make adjustments to ensure that workloads continue to operate smoothly without hitting the resource ceiling.

Adjusting ResourceQuotas

Resource quotas can be updated as the needs of the applications or teams change. Kubernetes allows administrators to modify the quota settings by simply updating the YAML configuration and applying the changes using Kubectl. However, it's important to do this carefully to avoid unnecessary disruption to running workloads. Quota updates should be made with an awareness of the current resource consumption and potential impacts on workloads within the namespace.

Assigning ResourceQuotas to namespaces is an essential practice for managing resource allocation in Kubernetes clusters. It ensures that resources are used efficiently and that no single namespace monopolises the available resources. By setting appropriate quotas, administrators can improve the stability, fairness, and cost-efficiency of the cluster. Regular monitoring and adjustment of quotas are crucial for maintaining optimal resource distribution and ensuring smooth operation across all namespaces.

6.3 Monitoring and Optimizing Resource Usage

Effective resource management in a Kubernetes cluster goes beyond just setting requests, limits, and quotas. Monitoring and optimizing resource usage are critical steps to ensure that the cluster remains efficient, cost-effective, and capable of handling workloads without over-provisioning or under-utilization of resources. This section delves into the importance of monitoring resource consumption, the tools available for it, and strategies for optimising resource usage to achieve a healthy and scalable Kubernetes environment.

Importance of Monitoring Resource Usage

Monitoring resource usage in a Kubernetes environment allows administrators to track the performance of applications and infrastructure, identify inefficiencies, and ensure that the resources allocated to workloads are being used effectively. By monitoring key metrics such as CPU, memory, storage, and network usage, administrators can make data-driven decisions to optimise resource allocation, identify bottlenecks, and prevent potential failures due to resource exhaustion. Without proper monitoring, teams may encounter issues like resource contention, application crashes, or degraded performance, all of which could lead to increased operational costs or downtime.

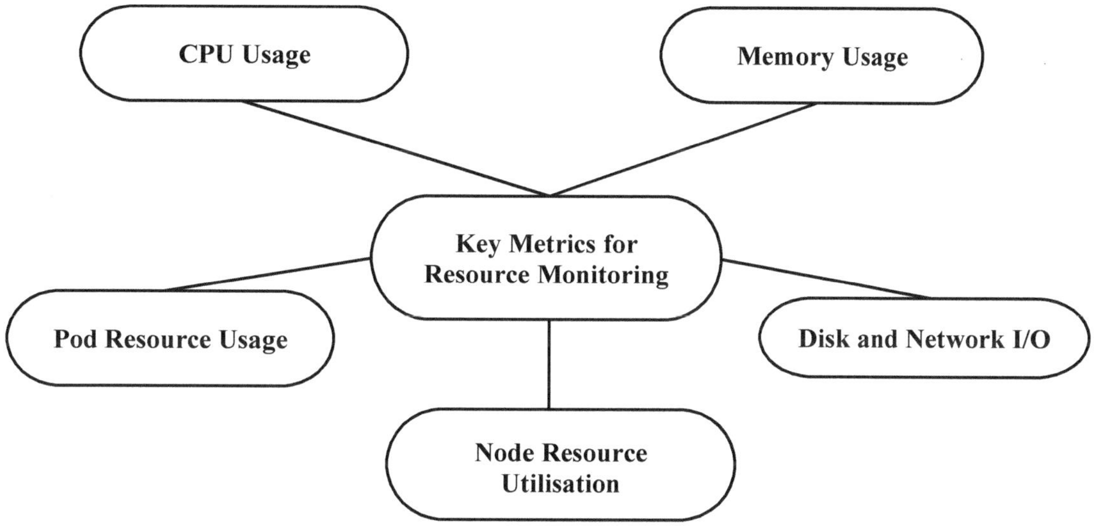

Key Metrics for Resource Monitoring

To effectively monitor resource usage, it's essential to track specific metrics that reflect the health and performance of applications. The most commonly monitored resources in a Kubernetes cluster include:

CPU Usage: Monitoring CPU usage helps ensure that applications are not consuming excessive processing power. Overuse of CPU can lead to throttling, while underuse indicates that resources are not being fully utilised.

Memory Usage: Memory consumption is another critical metric. Excessive memory usage can lead to out-of-memory (OOM) errors, where Kubernetes may kill and restart containers. On the other hand, underutilisation could indicate that resource limits are too high, potentially leading to wasted resources.

Pod Resource Usage: Since Kubernetes schedules Pods across nodes, tracking the resource usage of individual Pods helps identify Pods that are consuming too many resources or not using the allocated resources efficiently.

Disk and Network I/O: Monitoring storage and network usage provides insights into how workloads interact with persistent volumes and other networked services, ensuring there is no bottleneck that could affect application performance.

Node Resource Utilisation: Tracking resource utilisation at the node level is vital for detecting overburdened nodes and ensuring that workloads are distributed evenly across the cluster.

Tools for Monitoring Resource Usage

Kubernetes provides several built-in tools and third-party solutions to monitor resource usage in a cluster. Some of the most widely used tools include:

Kubernetes Metrics Server: The Metrics Server collects resource usage data from nodes and Pods and makes it available to Kubernetes components like the Horizontal Pod Autoscaler (HPA). The Metrics Server provides essential metrics like CPU and memory usage at the node and pod levels.

Prometheus and Grafana: Prometheus is a powerful open-source monitoring and alerting toolkit designed for Kubernetes. It collects metrics from various sources, including Kubernetes clusters, and stores them in a time-series database. Grafana is typically used in conjunction with Prometheus to visualise these metrics in interactive dashboards. This combination provides deep insights into the performance of both the cluster and individual applications.
Kubectl top: The kubectl top command is a simple way to get a snapshot of resource usage at the node and pod level. It pulls data from the Metrics Server and displays CPU and memory usage statistics for nodes and Pods in real-time.
Kube-state-metrics: Kube-state-metrics exposes detailed information about the state of Kubernetes objects, such as deployments, pods, and replicasets, which can be essential for gaining a deeper understanding of how resources are being used across the cluster.
Datadog, New Relic, and other APM tools: Application Performance Management (APM) tools like Datadog and New Relic provide comprehensive monitoring solutions that track application performance, resource utilisation, and overall system health. These tools offer advanced analytics and alerting features to help detect and resolve issues quickly.

Optimising Resource Usage

Once resource usage is being monitored, the next step is to optimise it. Efficient resource allocation helps prevent resource wastage, reduce operational costs, and improve the overall performance of the Kubernetes cluster. Several strategies can be employed to optimise resource usage:
Right-Sizing Resource Requests and Limits: One of the most effective ways to optimise resource usage is by accurately configuring resource requests and limits for containers. Underestimating these values can lead to resource exhaustion while overestimating them can result in wasted resources. Regularly analysing application performance and adjusting these values based on real-world data can help ensure optimal resource utilisation.
Horizontal Pod Autoscaling (HPA): Kubernetes provides the Horizontal Pod Autoscaler to automatically scale the number of pods in a deployment based on CPU or memory usage. By enabling HPA, you ensure that your application has the right number of replicas running to handle the load without over-consuming resources.
Vertical Pod Autoscaling (VPA): For workloads that experience fluctuating resource demands, Vertical Pod Autoscaler adjusts the CPU and memory requests for individual Pods. This is particularly useful for applications that may not require horizontal scaling but need varying resource levels over time.
Node Affinity and Taints/Tolerations: Administrators can use node affinity, taints, and tolerations to optimise resource distribution across the cluster. These mechanisms control where Pods are scheduled, ensuring that workloads are placed on the most appropriate nodes based on resource availability or other factors like hardware requirements.
Resource Quotas and Limits at Namespace Level: Setting resource quotas at the namespace level ensures that no single team or application consumes more than its fair share of resources. By limiting the total number of resources a namespace can use, Kubernetes helps prevent resource contention between different workloads.
Eviction Policies: Kubernetes uses eviction policies to manage resource contention when a node is under pressure. Containers that exceed their resource limits (e.g., memory or CPU) may be evicted to free up resources for higher-priority workloads. Fine-tuning eviction policies helps prevent unnecessary disruptions and ensures that critical applications are prioritised.
Efficient Use of Persistent Storage: Optimizing the usage of persistent volumes is another way to improve resource efficiency. Using storage classes, proper disk provisioning, and avoiding over-provisioning of storage resources can help manage disk usage more effectively.

Monitoring and optimising resource usage in Kubernetes is essential for ensuring that workloads are running efficiently without overloading the cluster or wasting resources. By leveraging the right monitoring tools and applying optimisation strategies, administrators can achieve a well-balanced and cost-effective Kubernetes environment. Continuous monitoring, coupled with intelligent adjustments to resource requests, limits, and scaling policies, helps maintain high performance and scalability while minimizing unnecessary resource consumption. Ultimately, the goal is to ensure that each application receives the resources it needs while maintaining the overall health and stability of the cluster.

6.4 Summary

Resource Requests: Defines the minimum amount of CPU and memory a container needs to run, ensuring it is scheduled on nodes with adequate resources.
Resource Limits: Specifies the maximum CPU and memory a container can use, preventing overconsumption that can negatively affect other containers on the node.
Request vs. Limit: Requests are used for scheduling, while limits control runtime resource usage; it's best to set requests lower than limits to allow for occasional spikes.
Tuning Resource Requests and Limits: Balancing requests and limits based on application performance and usage data is key to avoiding underutilization or overutilization.
ResourceQuotas: Limits the resources a namespace can consume (e.g., CPU, memory, pods), ensuring fair resource allocation across multiple teams or applications.
Monitoring and Optimizing Resources: Monitoring tools like Metrics Server, Prometheus, and kubectl top help track resource usage, while strategies like autoscaling, resource quotas, and efficient use of storage improve resource efficiency.

6.5 Glossary

Resource Request: The minimum amount of CPU and memory a container requires for operation, used by Kubernetes to schedule pods.
Resource Limit: The maximum amount of CPU and memory a container can use, ensuring it doesn't consume more than its share of resources.
ResourceQuota: A Kubernetes object that defines limits on the resources a namespace can consume, helping enforce fair usage across a cluster.
Horizontal Pod Autoscaler (HPA): A Kubernetes feature that automatically adjusts the number of pod replicas based on resource usage.
Vertical Pod Autoscaler (VPA): A Kubernetes tool that adjusts the CPU and memory resources for individual pods based on their needs.
Node Affinity: A Kubernetes scheduling rule that determines on which nodes a pod can be scheduled based on resource availability or other factors.
Eviction Policy: A Kubernetes policy that determines which pods to evict when a node is under resource pressure, prioritizing critical workloads.
Prometheus: An open-source monitoring tool used for collecting and querying metrics in a Kubernetes environment. Often paired with Grafana for visualisation.

Exercise

Exercise 1 - Choose the correct answer from the given options.

1. What is the primary purpose of setting resource requests and limits in Kubernetes?
a) To ensure high availability of Pods
b) To define the storage size for Pods
c) To control the CPU and memory usage of Pods
d) To assign roles to different users

2. Which of the following can be specified as a resource request for a Kubernetes container?
a) CPU
b) Memory

c) Disk storage
d) Both CPU and memory

Exercise 2 - Check if the sentence is true or false.

1. In Kubernetes, resource requests define the minimum amount of CPU and memory required for a container to run.

2. Setting resource limits in Kubernetes ensures that containers can consume unlimited CPU and memory resources.

Exercise 3 - Answer the following questions in your own words.

1. What is used to define the resource requirements for a pod?

2. What limits the maximum resources a pod can use?

Exercise 4 - Fill the blank space with the correct word.

1. In Kubernetes, resource ________ defines the minimum resources required by a pod, while resource limits define the maximum resources a pod can consume.

2. Resource requests ensure that Kubernetes ________ enough resources for a pod to run.

Exercise 5 - Match each word or phrase in Column A with Column B

1. Setting Resource Requests and Limits
2. Assigning Quotas to Namespaces
3. Monitoring Resource Usage
4. Optimizing Resource Usage
5. Namespace Quota Enforcement

a) Adjust configurations to improve resource efficiency.
b) Ensures Pods have guaranteed minimum and maximum resources.
c) Limits resource usage for a specific namespace.
d) Prevents users from exceeding allocated quotas.
e) Tracks the consumption of CPU, memory, and other resources.

Exercise 6 - The following questions consist of two statements: Assertion (A) and Reason (R). Answer these questions, selecting the appropriate options given below:

1. Assertion (A): Resource requests and limits are set in Kubernetes to ensure efficient allocation and prevent over-usage of resources.

Reason (R): Resource limits are optional and only provide guidance to Kubernetes in scheduling pods.

Alternatives:

a) Assertion (A) is true, and Reason (R) is the correct reason for Assertion (A).
b) Assertion (A) is true, but Reason (R) is not the correct reason for Assertion (A).
c) Assertion (A) is false, but Reason (R) is true.
d) Assertion (A) is true, but Reason (R) is false.

2. Assertion (A): Assigning quotas to namespaces helps prevent one team or application from consuming all resources in a Kubernetes cluster.

Reason (R): Resource quotas apply only to CPU and memory resources, but not to storage resources within a namespace.

Alternatives:

a) Assertion (A) is true, and Reason (R) is the correct reason for Assertion (A).

b) Assertion (A) is true, but Reason (R) is not the correct reason for Assertion (A).
c) Assertion (A) is false, but Reason (R) is true.
d) Assertion (A) is true, but Reason (R) is false.

Exercise 7 - Answer the following questions in 50 - 80 words.

1. What are resource requests and limits in Kubernetes?
2. How do resource requests help schedule pods in Kubernetes?

Exercise 8 - Answer the following questions in 100 - 120 words.

1. What are resource requests and limits in Kubernetes, and how do they help manage the allocation of CPU and memory resources to Pods?
2. Explain the difference between a resource request and a resource limit in Kubernetes. How do these settings affect the behaviour of containers in a Pod?

Answer

Exercise 1 - 1 c), 2 d).
Exercise 2 - 1 True, 2 False.
Exercise 3 - 1 Requests, 2 Limits.
Exercise 4 - 1 Requests, 2 Reserves.
Exercise 5 - 1 b), 2 c), 3 e), 4 a), 5 d).
Exercise 6 - 1 b), 2 d).

Online Resources

Online Exam Paper: https://forms.gle/eTi15JQwLeHcYZuh7

QR Code:

Chapter 7 - Security

Learning Objectives

Understand Role-Based Access Control (RBAC) and how to manage user access and permissions in Kubernetes.
Learn best practices for securing network communication between Pods and services within a Kubernetes cluster.
Explore methods to ensure container and Pod security by applying security policies and hardening techniques.
Gain insights into using security scanners to detect vulnerabilities and maintain a secure Kubernetes environment.

7.1 Role-based access control (RBAC)

Role-based Access Control (RBAC) is a widely adopted model for managing user permissions within a system based on their roles. It is a security mechanism that restricts system access to authorised users, ensuring that only individuals with the appropriate role can access certain resources or perform specific actions. In an RBAC system, users are assigned to roles, and roles are assigned to specific permissions, which define the actions that can be performed on resources.

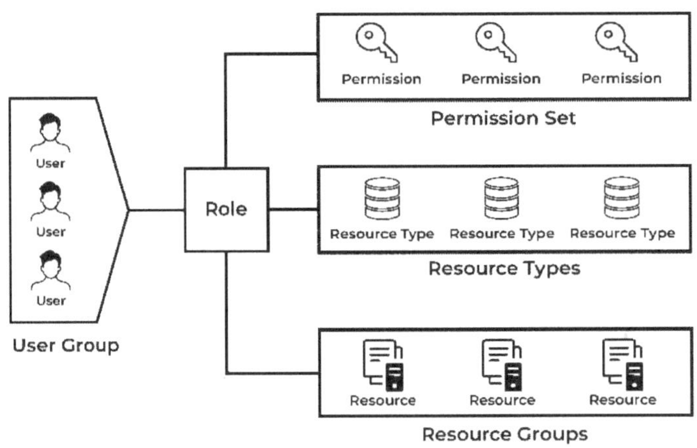

In RBAC, roles represent a collection of logically grouped permissions. For example, a system might have roles such as Admin, Manager, and Employee. The Admin role may have permissions to create, read, update, and delete all resources, while the Manager role might only have read and write access to specific resources, and the Employee role could have read-only access. The central idea is that users should be assigned roles based on their job responsibilities rather than individual permissions, making the management of access rights more efficient and scalable.

The primary advantage of RBAC is its simplicity and manageability. As the number of users and permissions in a system grows, managing access becomes more complex. However, by using roles, administrators can group users with similar access needs, reducing the need for individual permission assignments. This not only simplifies the administration of security policies but also reduces the likelihood of errors, as users are assigned roles rather than specific permissions.

Another key benefit of RBAC is its ability to enforce the principle of least privilege. By ensuring that users only have access to the resources necessary for their roles, RBAC minimizes the risk of unauthorised access or accidental misuse of sensitive data. For instance, if an employee needs to access only certain records, they will be granted a role with permissions that limit their access to those specific records, rather than giving them broad access to all data in the system.

RBAC also enhances compliance with regulatory requirements. Many standards and laws, such as the GDPR or HIPAA, require organisations to demonstrate that they have controlled access to sensitive information. RBAC provides a framework for implementing access control policies that help organisations meet these legal obligations. By clearly defining roles and permissions, organisations can provide evidence of how access to data is restricted and ensure that users only access information relevant to their responsibilities.

However, while RBAC offers significant advantages, it is not without limitations. One challenge is the potential complexity when roles need to be fine-tuned. As organisations grow, there may be a need for more granular control that RBAC may not inherently support. This can result in the need for additional mechanisms, such as Attribute-based Access Control (ABAC), which allows for more detailed policies based on attributes like user location or time of access.

Role-based Access Control (RBAC) is a crucial component of any modern security strategy, enabling organizations to effectively manage user access, enforce the principle of least privilege, and meet regulatory requirements. While RBAC offers simplicity and efficiency, it may require complementary mechanisms in complex environments where fine-grained access control is necessary.

7.2 Network Security

Network security is a critical aspect of protecting an organization's network infrastructure from unauthorized access, misuse, modification, or denial of service. It encompasses a wide range of policies, technologies, and practices aimed at safeguarding both hardware and software components of a network. The main goal of network security is to protect the confidentiality, integrity, and availability of data during transmission across the network, ensuring it remains secure and is not compromised by malicious actors.

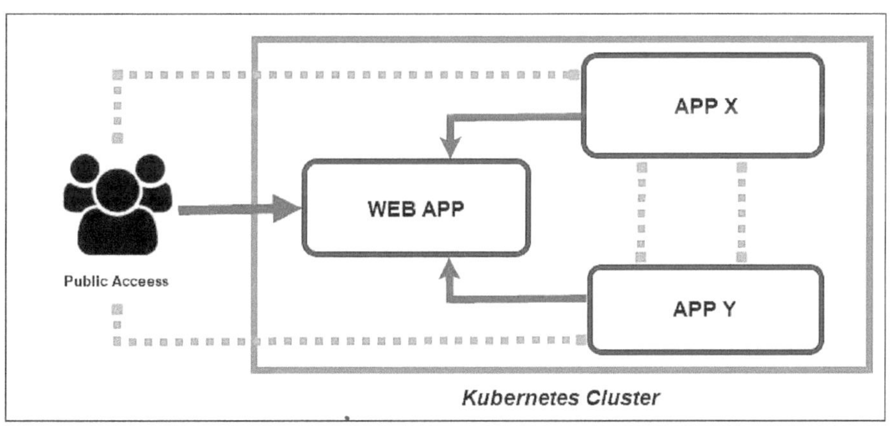

At its core, network security is designed to protect networks from cyberattacks, which can come in various forms, including viruses, malware, phishing, man-in-the-middle attacks, and Distributed Denial of Service (DDoS) attacks. These threats can have devastating consequences, ranging from data breaches and financial loss to reputational damage and operational disruptions. Therefore, robust network security practices are essential for both small and large enterprises to safeguard their assets, intellectual property, and sensitive information.

One of the foundational components of network security is the use of firewalls. Firewalls act as a barrier between a trusted internal network and untrusted external networks, filtering inbound and outbound traffic based on predefined security rules. By blocking unauthorised access and preventing potentially harmful traffic, firewalls help protect the network from external threats. Modern firewalls can be highly sophisticated, offering features such as intrusion detection, deep packet inspection, and application-level filtering to provide comprehensive protection.

In addition to firewalls, encryption plays a key role in securing network communications. Encryption converts data into an unreadable format, which can only be reverted to its original form with the correct decryption key. This ensures that even if data is intercepted during transmission, it cannot be accessed or altered by unauthorised individuals. Encryption is particularly important for securing sensitive information, such as login credentials, financial transactions, and personal data, as it provides an additional layer of protection against eavesdropping and tampering.

Virtual Private Networks (VPNs) are another important tool in network security, allowing users to establish a secure, encrypted connection over a less secure network, such as the internet. VPNs are commonly used by remote workers or individuals accessing corporate networks from external locations. By tunnelling traffic through a secure channel, VPNs ensure that data remains private and protected, even when transmitted over public networks.

Intrusion Detection and Prevention Systems (IDPS) are essential for detecting and responding to malicious activities in real time. IDPS tools monitor network traffic for signs of suspicious activity or known attack patterns, and can trigger alerts or automatically block certain traffic. These systems help security teams identify potential threats before they cause significant damage, enabling a swift response to mitigate risks.

Another crucial aspect of network security is implementing secure network architecture. This includes segmenting the network into smaller subnets or zones based on the sensitivity of the data they handle. By isolating critical systems and sensitive information from less secure parts of the network, organisations can limit the scope of potential attacks and reduce the attack surface. Additionally, network access controls, such as multi-factor authentication (MFA) and strong password policies, help ensure that only authorised individuals can access sensitive resources.

Regular monitoring and auditing are also essential practices in maintaining network security. By continuously monitoring network activity, administrators can identify and address vulnerabilities, misconfigurations, or emerging threats in a timely manner. Security Information and Event Management (SIEM) systems are often used for centralized logging and analysis of network events, enabling organisations to detect anomalies and perform forensic investigations when needed.

Network security is a multifaceted discipline that involves a combination of technical measures, policies, and practices designed to protect the integrity and confidentiality of data transmitted over a network. With the growing sophistication of cyber threats, organisations must adopt a layered security approach, utilising firewalls, encryption, VPNs, intrusion detection systems, and secure network architecture to safeguard their networks from attacks. Proactive monitoring and regular updates are essential to stay ahead of emerging threats and ensure a resilient network infrastructure.

7.3 Container and Pod Security

Container and pod security is a critical aspect of securing modern cloud-native applications, which often rely on containerised environments for efficient deployment, scaling, and management. Containers, such as those orchestrated by Kubernetes, package applications and their dependencies into isolated environments, ensuring consistency across development, testing, and production. Pods, which are the smallest deployable units in Kubernetes, encapsulate one or more containers along with their storage, network, and configuration specifications. While containers and pods offer significant benefits in terms of portability and scalability, they also introduce unique security challenges that must be addressed to protect the underlying infrastructure and sensitive data.

One of the primary concerns with container and pod security is ensuring that containers are free from vulnerabilities before they are deployed. Malicious code or security flaws within the container image can potentially expose the system to cyberattacks. It is essential to use trusted base images and regularly scan container images for known vulnerabilities using security scanning tools. Additionally, keeping containers up-to-date by applying security patches and updates is crucial in preventing attackers from exploiting outdated software components.

Another important aspect of container and pod security is isolating workloads to minimize the potential impact of a compromised container or pod. Containers share the underlying host system's kernel, which means that a vulnerability in one container could potentially affect others on the same host. To mitigate this risk, security best practices such as the use of namespaces, control groups (cgroups), and seccomp profiles can be implemented to limit the resources a container can access and the actions it can perform. Pod security policies (PSPs) in Kubernetes also play a crucial role in defining the security context in which pods run, restricting access to sensitive resources, and enforcing security controls such as running containers with non-root privileges.

In Kubernetes, role-based access control (RBAC) is a powerful security mechanism that controls who can access and modify resources within the cluster. By defining roles and assigning them to users, organisations can enforce the principle of least privilege, ensuring that only authorised users can access specific resources or perform sensitive operations. RBAC can be used to restrict access to pods, services, and other Kubernetes objects, reducing the attack surface and limiting the potential impact of a compromised user account.

Network security is another vital aspect of container and pod security. Containers and pods often communicate with each other within a Kubernetes cluster, and securing these communications is essential to prevent unauthorised access or data leakage. Network policies in Kubernetes allow administrators to define rules that control the flow of traffic between pods and external resources. By isolating communication paths and restricting access to sensitive services, network policies can help prevent lateral movement within the cluster in the event of a breach.

Runtime security is a dynamic aspect of container and pod security, focusing on monitoring and protecting containers while they are running. Runtime security tools can detect suspicious behaviour, such as abnormal system calls, unauthorised file access, or unexpected changes to the container filesystem. By continuously monitoring container activity, security teams can identify and respond to potential threats in real-time. Additionally, techniques like container image signing and runtime defence mechanisms help ensure that containers haven't been tampered with before or after deployment.

Logging and monitoring are essential practices for maintaining container and pod security. By enabling logging and collecting security-related metrics, organisations can gain visibility into container and pod activities, detect security incidents, and perform post-incident analysis. Centralised logging solutions, such as the Elastic Stack or Fluentd, can aggregate logs from various sources within the container ecosystem, making it easier to identify anomalies and correlate events across the infrastructure.

Lastly, securing the host environment is critical for ensuring the overall security of containers and pods. Since containers share the host system's kernel, any vulnerabilities in the host can potentially compromise all containers running on it. Securing the host involves implementing hardening measures, such as disabling unnecessary services, using minimal base images, and applying security patches regularly. Additionally, container runtimes, like Docker or containers, should be kept up to date, and security features like Docker Content Trust (DCT) should be enabled to prevent the use of unsigned or untrusted images.

Container and pod security is a multi-faceted challenge that requires a combination of preventative, detective, and responsive measures. By securing container images, isolating workloads, implementing network policies, monitoring runtime activity, and ensuring proper access control, organisations can significantly reduce the risk of security breaches in containerized environments. With the rapid adoption of containerisation and orchestration technologies like Kubernetes, it is essential for security practices to evolve alongside these advancements to protect cloud-native applications from emerging threats.

7.4 Security Scanners

Security scanners are essential tools in the modern cybersecurity landscape, designed to identify and address vulnerabilities within systems, applications, and networks. These scanners are critical for proactively detecting security weaknesses before attackers can exploit them. Security scanners come in various forms, such as network vulnerability scanners, static application security testing (SAST) tools, dynamic application security testing (DAST) tools, and container security scanners, each tailored to different layers of an organization's infrastructure. By scanning for known vulnerabilities, misconfigurations, or weaknesses in software components, security scanners help organizations maintain a strong security posture and comply with regulatory requirements.

One of the most common types of security scanners is the network vulnerability scanner, which scans networked systems for vulnerabilities that attackers could exploit. These tools typically look for outdated software, open ports, misconfigurations, and other weaknesses that could expose systems to remote attacks. Popular network vulnerability scanners, such as Nessus, OpenVAS, and Qualys, automate the process of discovering these vulnerabilities, making it easier for security teams to identify and patch issues before they can be exploited. Regular scanning of network assets is an essential practice to ensure that vulnerabilities are addressed promptly and that the network remains secure.

Static Application Security Testing (SAST) scanners are used to analyse the source code of applications for security vulnerabilities. These tools examine the codebase for issues like SQL injection, cross-site scripting (XSS), buffer overflows, and insecure coding practices. Since SAST scanners operate on the source code or binaries before the application is executed, they provide an early detection mechanism for vulnerabilities that could otherwise go unnoticed during runtime. SAST scanners are valuable for ensuring that applications are secure from the moment they are developed, enabling developers to fix issues before deployment.

Dynamic Application Security Testing (DAST) scanners, in contrast to SAST, focus on identifying vulnerabilities in running applications. These scanners simulate real-world attacks on web applications, APIs, and other running systems, testing how they respond to various threat scenarios. DAST scanners are particularly useful for identifying runtime vulnerabilities that may not be visible in static code analysis, such as input validation issues or authentication weaknesses. By scanning applications in their deployed environment, DAST tools help ensure that security flaws are detected before attackers can exploit them in production.

Container security scanners are specifically designed to identify vulnerabilities and misconfigurations in containerized environments, such as Docker or Kubernetes. These scanners check container images for known vulnerabilities, insecure configurations, and compliance issues, ensuring that only secure containers are deployed in production. Container security is a crucial part of the DevSecOps process, as containers are widely used for their portability and scalability. Tools like Clair, Trivy, and Anchore help automate the scanning of container images before they are deployed, minimizing the risk of introducing vulnerabilities into the production environment.

In addition to detecting vulnerabilities, security scanners also play a key role in compliance auditing. Many organisations are required to meet industry standards and regulatory requirements, such as PCI-DSS, HIPAA, or GDPR, which mandate specific security practices. Security scanners can automate the process of checking systems against these compliance requirements, ensuring that organisations remain aligned with legal and industry standards. Compliance-focused scanners can identify areas where security practices may be lacking or where systems do not meet the required security controls, helping organisations avoid potential fines or reputational damage.

The effectiveness of security scanners is significantly enhanced when integrated into the continuous integration and continuous deployment (CI/CD) pipeline. By incorporating security scanning into the development process, organisations can identify vulnerabilities early in the software development lifecycle, enabling quicker remediation and reducing the risk of vulnerabilities reaching production. This shift-left approach to security ensures that security is an integral part of the development workflow rather than a last-minute concern.

Despite their many benefits, security scanners are not foolproof and should not be relied upon as the sole defence mechanism. While they are excellent at identifying known vulnerabilities, they may not always catch new or emerging threats, zero-day vulnerabilities, or sophisticated attack techniques. As such, security scanners should be used in conjunction with other security measures, such as manual code reviews, penetration testing, and threat intelligence, to provide a comprehensive security strategy.

Security scanners are a vital tool in the arsenal of cybersecurity professionals, helping organisations identify and address vulnerabilities across a wide range of systems and applications. Whether used for scanning networks, applications, containers, or compliance requirements, security scanners enable organisations to proactively address security issues before they can be exploited. However, for maximum effectiveness, security scanners should be part of a broader security framework that includes both automated tools and human oversight, ensuring a well-rounded approach to cybersecurity.

7.5 Summary

RBAC (Role-Based Access Control): Manages user permissions based on roles to simplify access control and enforce the principle of least privilege.
Network Security: Protects networks from cyberattacks and unauthorized access, using tools like firewalls, VPNs, and intrusion detection systems.
Container and Pod Security: Secures containerized environments (like Kubernetes), focusing on trusted images, workload isolation, and runtime monitoring.
Security Scanners: Identify vulnerabilities in systems, applications, and containers, helping organizations detect issues before they can be exploited.
Compliance and Monitoring: Regular auditing, logging, and integration with CI/CD pipelines help maintain security and regulatory compliance.

7.6 Glossary

RBAC (Role-Based Access Control): A security model that assigns permissions to roles, simplifying access management.
Firewall: A network security system that filters traffic to block unauthorized access.
Encryption: The process of converting data into an unreadable format to prevent unauthorized access.
DAST (Dynamic Application Security Testing): A security test that identifies vulnerabilities in running applications.
Container Security: Secures containers and pods by using trusted images, isolation techniques, and runtime monitoring.

Exercise

Exercise 1 - Choose the correct answer from the given options.

1. What is the main purpose of Role-Based Access Control (RBAC) in Kubernetes?
a) To control network traffic between Pods
b) To define and manage user access to Kubernetes resources
c) To manage container storage
d) To monitor resource usage in the cluster

2. Which Kubernetes object is used to define a set of permissions for a user or group in RBAC?
a) Pod
b) ServiceAccount
c) Role or ClusterRole
d) Namespace

Exercise 2 - Check if the sentence is true or false.

1. Role-based access control (RBAC) in Kubernetes allows administrators to define and control access to resources based on roles.
2. RBAC in Kubernetes allows users to define permissions for specific containers and pods, but not for other Kubernetes resources.

Exercise 3 - Answer the following questions in your own words.

1. What manages permissions and access within Kubernetes?
2. What ensures secure communication between services in Kubernetes?

Exercise 4 - Fill the blank space with the correct word.

1. ________ is a method used to control who can perform actions on resources within a Kubernetes cluster.

2. In Kubernetes, ________ allows the assignment of roles and permissions to users or groups based on their responsibilities.

Exercise 5 - Match each word or phrase in Column A with Column B

1. Role-based access control (RBAC)
2. Network Security
3. Container and Pod Security
4. Security Scanners
5. Kubernetes Secrets Encryption

a) Secures sensitive data stored in Kubernetes Secrets.
b) Ensures container isolation and prevents unauthorised access.
c) Detects vulnerabilities in images, code, and dependencies.
d) Restrict user actions based on defined roles.
e) Controls traffic between Pods, namespaces, and external sources.

Exercise 6 - The following questions consist of two statements: Assertion (A) and Reason (R). Answer these questions, selecting the appropriate options given below:

1. Assertion (A): Role-based access control (RBAC) in Kubernetes ensures that users and services only have access to the necessary resources.

Reason (R): RBAC only provides access to specific resources but does not allow fine-grained control over actions such as read or write.

Alternatives:

a) Assertion (A) is true, and Reason (R) is the correct reason for Assertion (A).
b) Assertion (A) is true, but Reason (R) is not the correct reason for Assertion (A).
c) Assertion (A) is false, but Reason (R) is true.
d) Assertion (A) is true, but Reason (R) is false.

2. Assertion (A): Network security in Kubernetes can be enhanced by using network policies to control communication between pods.

Reason (R): Network policies enforce access control by defining how pods and external resources can communicate with each other.

Alternatives:

a) Assertion (A) is true, and Reason (R) is the correct reason for Assertion (A).
b) Assertion (A) is true, but Reason (R) is not the correct reason for Assertion (A).
c) Assertion (A) is false, but Reason (R) is true.
d) Assertion (A) is true, but Reason (R) is false.

Exercise 7 - Answer the following questions in 50 - 80 words.

1. What is Role-Based Access Control (RBAC) in Kubernetes?

2. How does RBAC manage access to resources in a Kubernetes cluster?

Exercise 8 - Answer the following questions in 100 - 120 words.

1. What is Role-Based Access Control (RBAC) in Kubernetes, and how does it help manage permissions for users and applications in a cluster?

2. Explain how Kubernetes RBAC works. What are the key components of an RBAC policy, and how are roles and role bindings configured?

Answer

Exercise 1 - 1 b), 2 c).
Exercise 2 - 1 True, 2 False.
Exercise 3 - 1 RBAC, 2 Network.
Exercise 4 - 1 RBAC, 2 RBAC.
Exercise 5 - 1 d), 2 e), 3 b), 4 c), 5 a).
Exercise 6 - 1 b), 2 a).

Online Resources

Online Exam Paper: https://forms.gle/rpjRCnpvKyxYJqB47

QR Code:

Chapter 8 – Monitoring and Logging

Learning Objectives
Understand how to access and analyse logs from Kubernetes Pods and system components for troubleshooting.
Learn how to collect and monitor metrics to track the performance and health of applications and clusters.
Explore the use of distributed tracing to gain insights into application workflows and latency issues.
Gain knowledge of tools and techniques for implementing effective logging and monitoring in Kubernetes.
Understand the role of logs, metrics, and traces in maintaining a reliable and observable Kubernetes environment.

8.1 Logs

Logs are fundamental components of any monitoring and logging system, providing valuable insights into the operations, performance, and security of applications, systems, and networks. They are records generated by software applications, services, or hardware devices that capture key events, transactions, and activities that occur within a system. Logs are essential for troubleshooting issues, detecting security breaches, monitoring system health, and ensuring compliance with regulatory standards. By capturing detailed information about system operations, logs provide a historical record that can be used for analysis, audits, and forensic investigations.

In a typical system, logs can include a wide range of information, such as timestamps, event types, error messages, user activities, and system performance metrics. For example, a web server might log every HTTP request it processes, including details such as the client's IP address, requested URL, response status code, and the time taken to fulfill the request. Similarly, application logs may capture information about database queries, application errors, or warnings that could indicate performance issues. System logs can record information related to operating system activities, hardware status, network connections, and security events.

The importance of logs extends beyond their utility in troubleshooting and diagnostics. Logs play a critical role in security monitoring by providing detailed records of system activities that can be analysed for signs of malicious behaviour or security incidents. For instance, logs can help identify unauthorised access attempts, suspicious file modifications, privilege escalations, and unusual patterns of network traffic. By integrating logs with security information and event management (SIEM) systems, organisations can correlate log data from various sources to detect potential threats and respond to security incidents in real-time.

Another vital aspect of logs is their role in regulatory compliance. Many industries are subject to strict regulatory frameworks, such as GDPR, HIPAA, or PCI-DSS, which mandate the collection, storage, and management of log data to ensure the integrity and security of sensitive information. Logs are often required to be retained for a specific period and must be accessible for auditing and forensic investigations. For example, financial institutions must log and retain access to customer transactions to demonstrate compliance with anti-money laundering (AML) regulations. By ensuring that logs are properly collected and stored, organisations can fulfill compliance requirements and avoid potential penalties.

Log management, which involves collecting, aggregating, storing, and analysing logs, is a crucial practice for maintaining effective monitoring and logging systems. As systems become more complex and distributed, managing logs from multiple sources becomes increasingly challenging. Centralised log management platforms, such as Elasticsearch, Splunk, or the ELK stack (Elasticsearch, Logstash, and Kibana), provide a way to aggregate and analyse logs from various systems in one place. These platforms often include powerful search, filtering, and visualisation tools that allow security teams, system administrators, and developers to analyse log data efficiently and gain insights into system health and security posture.

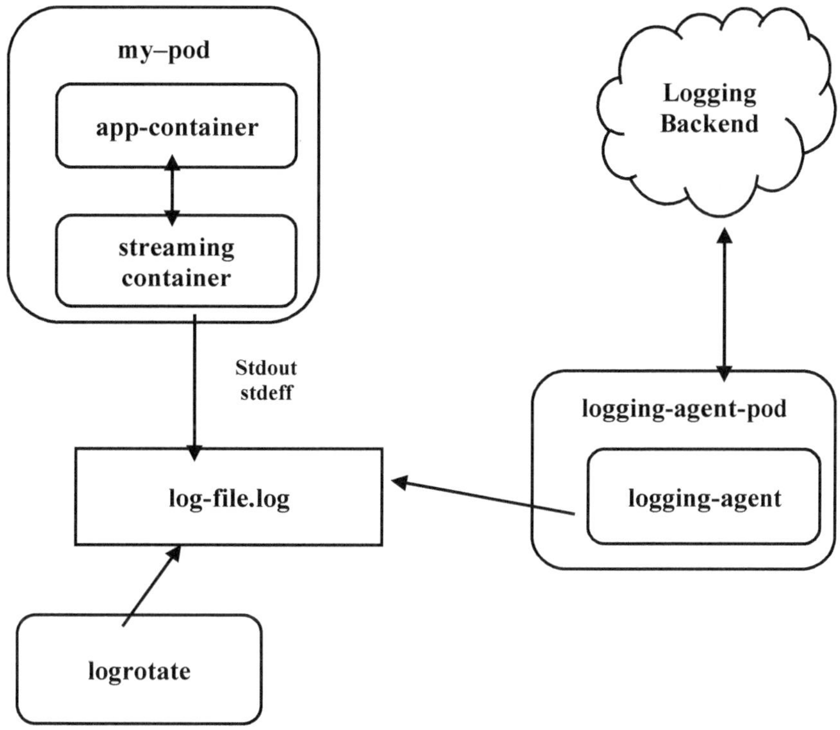

Log aggregation is particularly important in distributed systems, where logs from multiple servers, containers, or microservices need to be consolidated for a holistic view of the environment. In Kubernetes-based systems, for example, logs from different containers and pods need to be collected and centralized to track the overall performance and security of the application. By using log aggregation tools, organisations can reduce the noise of managing logs from multiple sources and streamline the process of analysing large volumes of data.

Effective log retention policies are also crucial for managing the lifecycle of logs. While logs provide significant value, they can quickly accumulate, leading to storage challenges and potential performance issues. Organisations need to implement strategies for archiving, rotating, or deleting old logs to ensure that storage resources are used efficiently while maintaining compliance with retention requirements. Retention policies should take into account the type of log, the retention period required by regulations, and the organisation's internal needs for auditing and investigations.

Analysing logs is central to effective monitoring. Log analysis allows organisations to identify trends, detect anomalies, and uncover hidden patterns that may indicate issues or opportunities for optimisation. Advanced log analytics tools often employ machine learning algorithms to automatically detect deviations from normal behaviour, reducing the need for manual inspection of log data. These tools can trigger alerts based on predefined thresholds or anomalous events, enabling timely responses to potential system failures or security incidents.

Logs are indispensable tools for monitoring and managing the health, performance, and security of systems and applications. By capturing detailed records of system events, logs provide valuable insights for troubleshooting, compliance, security monitoring, and performance optimisation. Effective log management practices, including aggregation, analysis, and retention, ensure that organisations can efficiently handle and derive value from their log data, improving their ability to detect issues, respond to threats, and maintain a secure and compliant environment.

8.2 Metrics

Metrics play a vital role in monitoring the performance, health, and behaviour of systems, applications, and infrastructure. Unlike logs, which record specific events or activities, metrics are quantitative data that measure specific aspects of system performance over time. These can include various performance indicators such as CPU utilisation, memory usage, disk I/O, network bandwidth, response time, throughput, error rates, and other critical parameters that reflect the operational state of a system. By continuously collecting and analysing metrics, organisations can gain valuable insights into how their systems are performing and identify potential issues before they become critical.

One of the key advantages of metrics is that they provide a continuous, real-time view of a system's performance. While logs are typically generated when specific events occur, metrics are gathered at regular intervals, allowing teams to monitor trends and patterns over time. This makes metrics particularly useful for tracking the overall health and performance of an application or infrastructure, as well as for detecting anomalies or degradations in performance. For example, an increase in response time or a sudden spike in CPU usage may indicate a performance bottleneck or an impending failure, allowing teams to take proactive measures before the system becomes unresponsive or unstable.

Metrics are often organised into a time-series format, where each data point corresponds to a specific timestamp. This structure enables easy visualisation and comparison of performance over time, helping to identify trends or patterns. For example, a graph of CPU utilisation over the past 24 hours can reveal periods of peak usage, helping administrators identify which times of day the system is under the most strain. Time-series data can also be used to establish baselines, allowing teams to identify deviations from normal behaviour, such as sudden spikes in error rates or drops in system performance.

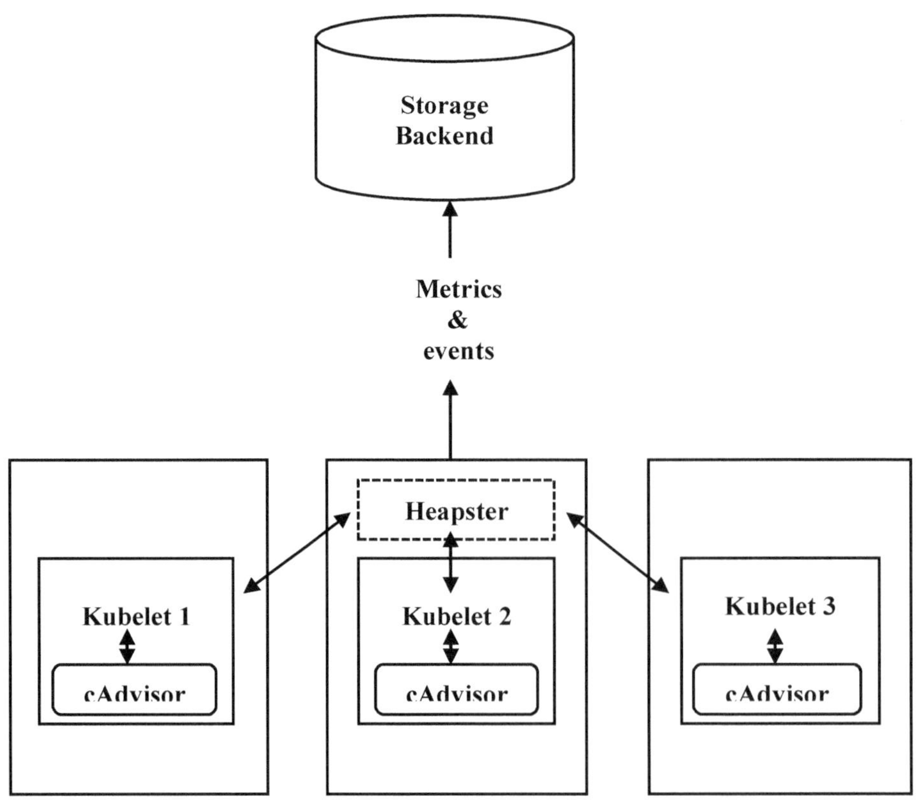

In the context of modern distributed systems, metrics are particularly important for monitoring applications and infrastructure that span multiple servers, containers, or microservices. In such environments, individual components must be monitored for their health and performance, and metrics provide a way to track how they are functioning in isolation and as part of the overall system. Tools like Prometheus, Datadog, and Grafana are widely used to collect, store, and visualise metrics across complex systems, allowing administrators to monitor the performance of each component and the system as a whole.

Metrics are not only useful for operational monitoring but also play a crucial role in capacity planning and optimization. By analysing historical metrics, organisations can gain insights into resource usage trends and predict future needs. For example, by tracking memory usage and CPU consumption over time, organisations can estimate when additional resources may be needed or when it might be time to scale the system. This predictive capability helps to optimise infrastructure usage and ensure that resources are allocated efficiently, preventing overprovisioning or under-provisioning of resources.

Another essential application of metrics is in alerting and automated responses. By setting thresholds for certain metrics, teams can configure alerting systems to notify them when performance deviates from expected values. For example, if CPU usage exceeds 90% for an extended period, an alert can be triggered, prompting administrators to investigate potential issues. Some advanced monitoring systems even integrate with automated remediation tools to take corrective actions based on metric values. For example, if network traffic exceeds a predefined threshold, the system could automatically scale out additional instances to handle the load.

Metrics also play an essential role in optimising the performance of applications and systems. By continuously collecting performance metrics, teams can identify areas for improvement and fine-tune their systems to operate more efficiently. For example, tracking response time and latency metrics can help developers identify slow database queries or inefficient algorithms that need to be optimised. In this way, metrics provide an ongoing feedback loop that helps organisations continuously improve their systems and applications, ensuring they operate at peak performance.

Metrics are a crucial element of monitoring and logging, providing real-time, quantitative insights into system performance and health. By continuously tracking key performance indicators, organisations can detect issues early, optimise system resources, and ensure the reliability and stability of their infrastructure and applications. Whether used for operational monitoring, capacity planning, alerting, or performance optimisation, metrics offer valuable data that helps organisations maintain efficient, high-performing systems while preventing issues before they impact users or business operations.

8.3 Traces

Traces are essential to monitoring and logging that provide detailed insights into the flow and execution of requests or transactions across distributed systems. Unlike logs and metrics, which focus on recording events and quantitative data, traces capture the journey of a request or transaction as it moves through various system components. This includes the individual steps, latencies, and interactions between microservices, databases, or external APIs. Traces are particularly valuable in modern, microservices-based architectures, where applications consist of numerous loosely coupled services that need to work together to fulfill a single user request.

A trace typically consists of multiple spans, where each span represents a unit of work or a specific operation that occurs during the execution of a request. Each span is assigned a unique identifier and contains information about the operation, such as the name of the service, the start and end times, and any relevant metadata. By connecting multiple spans together, traces can visualize the entire lifecycle of a request, from initiation to completion, allowing teams to understand the flow and identify bottlenecks or failures at specific stages. This level of granularity makes traces particularly useful for debugging complex, distributed systems where traditional logging and metrics might not provide enough context to diagnose issues effectively.

In distributed systems, especially those using microservices, a single user request may span multiple services, databases, or even external third-party APIs. Tracing allows for the correlation of events across these different components, helping teams understand how individual parts of the system interact and where potential problems might arise. For example, suppose a user is experiencing slow response times. In that case, traces can show the specific microservices or external dependencies that are contributing to the latency, enabling faster identification and resolution of the issue. This visibility across the entire request path is crucial for improving the performance and reliability of complex systems.

One of the primary benefits of traces is their ability to uncover performance bottlenecks and latency issues. By analysing the time spent on each span and understanding the overall request flow, teams can pinpoint areas where the system is lagging or where excessive time is spent. For instance, a trace may reveal that a specific database query is taking longer than expected or that communication between two services is causing delays. Identifying such performance bottlenecks allows teams to take corrective actions, such as optimising queries, improving service communication, or scaling specific components to handle increased load.

Traces are also helpful in troubleshooting and root cause analysis. When an error or failure occurs, traces provide a detailed view of the sequence of events leading up to the issue. This can help development and operations teams quickly identify the root cause, whether it's a misconfigured service, a bug in the code, or a network failure. With traces, teams can reduce the time it takes to resolve issues, as they have a clear and actionable view of the problem rather than relying on fragmented logs or isolated metrics.

In addition to their troubleshooting capabilities, traces contribute to enhancing observability within a system. Observability is the practice of understanding and monitoring the internal workings of a system based on the data it produces. Tracing enables teams to gain deeper insights into how a system behaves in real-world conditions, providing visibility into the flow of data and control across distributed services. This level of observability helps teams maintain control over complex, dynamic environments, ensuring that they can quickly detect anomalies and understand the system's behaviour under different conditions.

Modern distributed tracing tools, such as Jaeger, Zipkin, and OpenTelemetry, provide robust platforms for collecting, storing, and analysing traces across large-scale environments. These tools typically offer features like trace visualisation, which allows users to see the complete path of a request, including the latency between services and the duration of each span. Some tracing tools also integrate with other monitoring and logging systems, such as metrics and logs, creating a unified observability solution that combines traces with other data points to provide a holistic view of system performance.

To effectively utilise traces, organisations need to ensure that tracing is implemented consistently across their services. This involves instrumenting applications and services with tracing libraries or agents that can generate trace data for each request. It's important to maintain a balance between collecting sufficient trace data for observability and ensuring minimal performance overhead, as excessive tracing or detailed data collection can impact system performance. Organisations should also ensure that sensitive information is not exposed in trace data, implementing proper data sanitisation and masking practices to protect user privacy and comply with regulatory requirements.

Traces are a powerful tool for monitoring and logging in distributed systems, offering detailed insights into the flow and performance of requests as they traverse multiple services. By capturing spans of work and correlating them across the system, traces provide deep visibility into the interactions and potential bottlenecks that affect system performance. Tracing helps organisations troubleshoot issues faster, improve performance, and maintain robust observability in complex architectures. When combined with logs and metrics, traces form an essential part of a comprehensive monitoring strategy that helps ensure modern applications and services' reliability, performance, and security.

8.4 Summary

Logs: Records generated by software or hardware capturing system events, transactions, and activities, aiding in troubleshooting, security monitoring, and compliance.
Types of Logs: Include system logs (OS activities, hardware status), application logs (errors, database queries), and security logs (unauthorised access attempts, suspicious activities).
Log Management: Involves aggregating, storing, and analysing logs to ensure effective monitoring and compliance. Tools like ELK stack and Splunk help centralize log management.
Metrics: Quantitative data collected at regular intervals to measure system performance (e.g., CPU usage, memory, response time), aiding in capacity planning, alerting, and performance optimization.
Traces: Provide detailed insights into the execution flow of requests across microservices and components, helping diagnose performance bottlenecks and errors in distributed systems.
Tools for Tracing: Jaeger, Zipkin, and OpenTelemetry are popular tools for collecting and analysing traces across large-scale environments, offering enhanced observability.

8.5 Glossary

Logs: Records of system events, transactions, and activities that provide insights into system operations, health, and security.
Metrics: Quantitative data used to monitor system performance over time (e.g., CPU utilization, memory usage).
Traces: Detailed records of a request's journey through a system, capturing each operation or interaction between services.
Span: A unit of work or operation in a trace, representing an individual action or service call.
Distributed Tracing: A method for tracking and analysing requests as they move across multiple microservices or system components.
SIEM (Security Information and Event Management): A system used for real-time analysis of security alerts generated by applications and network hardware.
ELK Stack: A collection of three open-source tools (Elasticsearch, Logstash, Kibana) used for managing and analysing large volumes of log data.
Prometheus: A monitoring and alerting toolkit for time-series data, commonly used to collect and visualise metrics in distributed systems.

Exercise

Exercise 1 - Choose the correct answer from the given options.

1. What is the main purpose of logging in Kubernetes?
a) To manage resource allocation
b) To record detailed events and outputs of containerised applications
c) To scale applications automatically
d) To control network traffic between Pods

2. Which Kubernetes component is commonly used to collect and manage logs from Pods?
a) kubelet
b) kube-apiserver
c) Fluentd
d) Prometheus

Exercise 2 - Check if the sentence is true or false.

1. Logs in Kubernetes provide detailed information about the state and behaviour of applications running within the cluster.

2. Metrics in Kubernetes are used to track the performance and resource usage of containers, pods, and nodes.

Exercise 3 - Answer the following questions in your own words.

1. What records events and activities in a system?

2. What measures the performance and resource usage of Kubernetes?

Exercise 4 - Fill the blank space with the correct word.

1. ________ in Kubernetes captures detailed information about events, errors, and application output.

2. Kubernetes uses ________ to collect and store time-series data related to resource usage, such as CPU and memory.

Exercise 5 - Match each word or phrase in Column A with Column B

1. Logs
2. Metrics
3. Traces
4. Log Aggregation Tools
5. Alerting Systems

a) Tracks quantitative data like CPU usage and memory consumption.
b) Collects and centralises logs from multiple sources.
c) Captures detailed event data from applications and services.
d) Notifies users of critical issues based on metrics and logs.
e) Tracks the flow of requests across distributed systems.

Exercise 6 - The following questions consist of two statements: Assertion (A) and Reason (R). Answer these questions, selecting the appropriate options given below:

1. Assertion (A): Logs are crucial for debugging and troubleshooting issues in Kubernetes clusters.

Reason (R): Logs only provide real-time information about system events and do not store historical data for future analysis.

Alternatives:

a) Assertion (A) is true, and Reason (R) is the correct reason for Assertion (A).
b) Assertion (A) is true, but Reason (R) is not the correct reason for Assertion (A).
c) Assertion (A) is false, but Reason (R) is true.
d) Assertion (A) is true, but Reason (R) is false.

2. Assertion (A): Metrics in Kubernetes help monitor the health and performance of applications running in the cluster.

Reason (R): Metrics are only useful for tracking application errors and cannot be used to measure resource usage or performance.

Alternatives:

a) Assertion (A) is true, and Reason (R) is the correct reason for Assertion (A).
b) Assertion (A) is true, but Reason (R) is not the correct reason for Assertion (A).
c) Assertion (A) is false, but Reason (R) is true.
d) Assertion (A) is true, but Reason (R) is false.

Exercise 7 - Answer the following questions in 50 - 80 words.

1. What is the purpose of logging in Kubernetes?

2. How are logs typically generated and stored in a Kubernetes cluster?

Exercise 8 - Answer the following questions in 100 - 120 words.

1. What is the importance of logging in Kubernetes, and how can logs help troubleshoot and monitor applications running in a Kubernetes cluster?
2. Describe the different types of logs generated in a Kubernetes environment. How can you collect and manage logs for containers, Pods, and nodes?

Answer

Exercise 1 - 1 b), 2 c).
Exercise 2 - 1 True, 2 True.
Exercise 3 - 1 Logs, 2 Metrics.
Exercise 4 - 1 Metrics, 2 Metrics.
Exercise 5 - 1 c), 2 a), 3 e), 4 b), 5 d).
Exercise 6 - 1 b), 2 d).

Online Resources

Online Exam Paper: https://forms.gle/of5PJNbFApvDivYc8

QR Code:

Chapter 9 - Autoscaling

Learning Objectives

Understand the concept of Horizontal Pod Autoscaler (HPA) and how it adjusts the number of Pods based on resource utilization.

Learn about Vertical Pod Autoscaler (VPA) and its role in dynamically adjusting resource requests and limits for Pods.

Explore Cluster Autoscaling and how it scales the number of nodes in a Kubernetes cluster to meet workload demands.

Gain insights into configuring and fine-tuning autoscaling mechanisms to optimize performance and cost.

Understand the interplay between HPA, VPA, and Cluster Autoscaling in managing scalability in Kubernetes.

9.1 Horizontal Pod Autoscaler (HPA)

The Horizontal Pod Autoscaler (HPA) is a Kubernetes resource that automatically adjusts the number of pods in a deployment, replica set, or stateful set based on observed metrics like CPU or memory utilisation. This feature is essential for ensuring that applications can dynamically scale to meet workload demands while optimizing resource utilization.

How HPA Works

The HPA controller, which runs as part of the Kubernetes control plane, periodically queries the Kubernetes Metrics Server for the current resource utilization metrics of pods. Based on a defined target metric value, such as average CPU utilization, the HPA controller calculates the desired number of pods required to handle the workload efficiently. If the current number of pods differs from the calculated number, the HPA updates the deployment or replica set to match the desired state.

For example, consider a deployment with a target CPU utilization of 50%. If the average CPU utilization exceeds this threshold, the HPA scales up the number of pods. Conversely, if the utilization falls below the target, the HPA scales down the pods to save resources.

Configuration of HPA

To configure HPA, you need to create a HorizontalPodAutoscaler resource using a YAML file or kubectl command. The configuration specifies the following key parameters:

Target Deployment: The name of the deployment or replica set to be scaled.

Metrics: The metric type (e.g., CPU, memory, or custom metrics) and target value for scaling decisions.

Min and Max Pods: The minimum and maximum number of pods the HPA can scale to.

An example YAML configuration for HPA:

```
apiVersion: autoscaling/v2
kind: HorizontalPodAutoscaler
metadata:
  name: example-hpa
spec:
  scaleTargetRef:
    apiVersion: apps/v1
    kind: Deployment
    name: example-deployment
  minReplicas: 1
  maxReplicas: 10
  metrics:
    - type: Resource
      resource:
        name: cpu
        target:
          type: Utilization
   averageUtilization: 50
```

This configuration ensures that the example deployment scales between 1 and 10 pods based on CPU utilization.

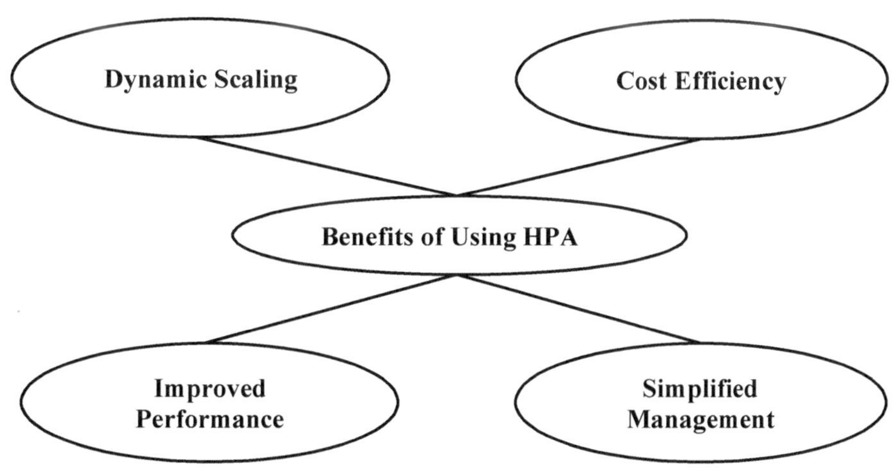

Benefits of Using HPA

Dynamic Scaling: HPA enables applications to handle varying traffic patterns effectively by scaling up during peak demand and scaling down during idle periods.

Cost Efficiency: By optimising the number of running pods, HPA reduces cloud resource costs.

Improved Performance: Autoscaling ensures that applications remain responsive even during high traffic.

Simplified Management: Developers and operators can focus on application logic without worrying about manual scaling.

Challenges and Considerations

While HPA provides significant advantages, it comes with challenges. For instance:

Metrics Availability: HPA relies on the Kubernetes Metrics Server, which must be properly configured and running.

Latency: Scaling decisions are not instantaneous, leading to potential delays in response to rapid workload changes.

Custom Metrics: Setting up and monitoring custom application-specific metrics can be complex.

Despite these challenges, the Horizontal Pod Autoscaler remains a vital tool for managing workloads in Kubernetes environments. It is a cornerstone of cloud-native application scaling, providing both flexibility and reliability.

9.2 Vertical Pod Autoscaler (VPA)

The Vertical Pod Autoscaler (VPA) is a Kubernetes tool designed to optimise the resource allocation of individual pods by automatically adjusting their CPU and memory requests and limits. This adjustment ensures that applications have sufficient resources to perform efficiently without over-provisioning, thus reducing wasted resources.

How VPA Works

Unlike the Horizontal Pod Autoscaler, which modifies the number of pods, the VPA focuses on resizing the resources allocated to each pod. The VPA recommender component monitors the resource usage of pods over time and calculates optimal resource settings. Based on these recommendations, it can:

Update Resource Requests and Limits: VPA adjusts the CPU and memory requests in the pod specifications.

Evict Pods (Optional): To apply the new resource settings, the VPA may evict existing pods, allowing them to restart with the updated configuration.

VPA operates in three modes:

Off: Recommendations are generated but not applied.

Auto: Recommendations are automatically applied, and pods are restarted if necessary.

Initial: Recommendations are applied only when pods are first created.

Configuration of VPA

Configuring a VPA involves defining a VerticalPodAutoscaler resource in YAML. Key parameters include the target deployment, update policy, and resource recommendations. Below is an example configuration:

```
apiVersion: autoscaling.k8s.io/v1
kind: VerticalPodAutoscaler
metadata:
  name: example-vpa
spec:
  targetRef:
    apiVersion: apps/v1
    kind: Deployment
    name: example-deployment
  updatePolicy:
updateMode: "Auto"
```

This configuration ensures that the example deployment automatically adjusts CPU and memory resources based on usage patterns.

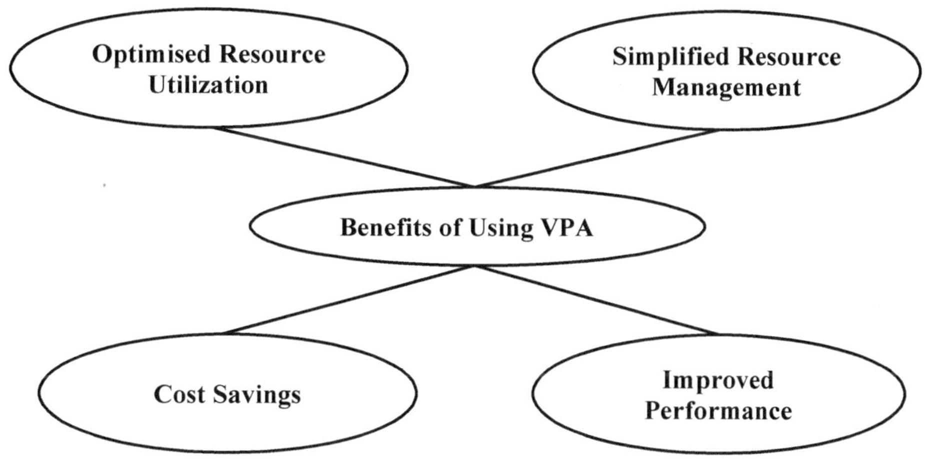

Benefits of Using VPA
Optimised Resource Utilization: VPA ensures that pods have the right amount of resources, preventing both under- and over-provisioning.
Simplified Resource Management: Developers can focus on application logic without manually tuning resource requests and limits.
Cost Savings: By reducing resource wastage, VPA lowers infrastructure costs.
Improved Performance: Applications run more efficiently with correctly allocated resources.

Challenges and Considerations
While VPA is a powerful tool, it has some limitations and considerations:
Pod Evictions: Resource updates may require evicting pods, potentially disrupting running applications.
Compatibility with HPA: Using VPA alongside HPA can lead to conflicts, as they target different scaling dimensions.
Initial Resource Settings: Proper initial resource settings are crucial to avoid performance bottlenecks before VPA recommendations take effect.

The Vertical Pod Autoscaler complements Kubernetes' autoscaling capabilities by focusing on resource optimisation at the pod level. It plays a crucial role in maintaining application performance and cost-efficiency in dynamic cloud environments.

9.3 Cluster Autoscaling

The Cluster Autoscaler is a Kubernetes component designed to manage the scaling of worker nodes in a cluster. It ensures that the cluster has sufficient capacity to handle the workload by adding nodes when resources are insufficient and removing underutilised nodes to save costs. This feature is particularly useful in dynamic environments with fluctuating workloads.

How Cluster Autoscaler Works
The Cluster Autoscaler monitors pending pods that cannot be scheduled due to resource constraints. When it detects such pods, it evaluates the cluster's current capacity and works with the underlying infrastructure provider

to provision additional nodes. Conversely, if it identifies underutilised nodes and can have their workloads moved to other nodes, it scales down by terminating these nodes.
For example, if a workload requires more memory than any existing node can provide, the Cluster Autoscaler adds a new node with sufficient resources. Similarly, if a node's pods can be rescheduled elsewhere, the node is terminated to reduce costs.

Configuration of Cluster Autoscaler
To enable the Cluster Autoscaler, you need to configure it based on the cloud provider's implementation (e.g., AWS, GCP, Azure). Common parameters include:
Node Group: Defines the set of nodes managed by the autoscaler.
Scaling Limits: Specifies the minimum and maximum number of nodes allowed in the cluster.
Resource Constraints: Ensures that nodes meet specific resource requirements for workloads.

Below is an example of configuring Cluster Autoscaler using Kubernetes:

```
apiVersion: cluster.k8s.io/v1alpha1
kind: ClusterAutoscaler
metadata:
  name: example-cluster-autoscaler
spec:
  scaleTargetRef:
    apiVersion: apps/v1
    kind: NodeGroup
    name: example-node-group
  minNodes: 1
  maxNodes: 10
```

This configuration ensures that the example-node-group can scale between 1 and 10 nodes based on workload demands.

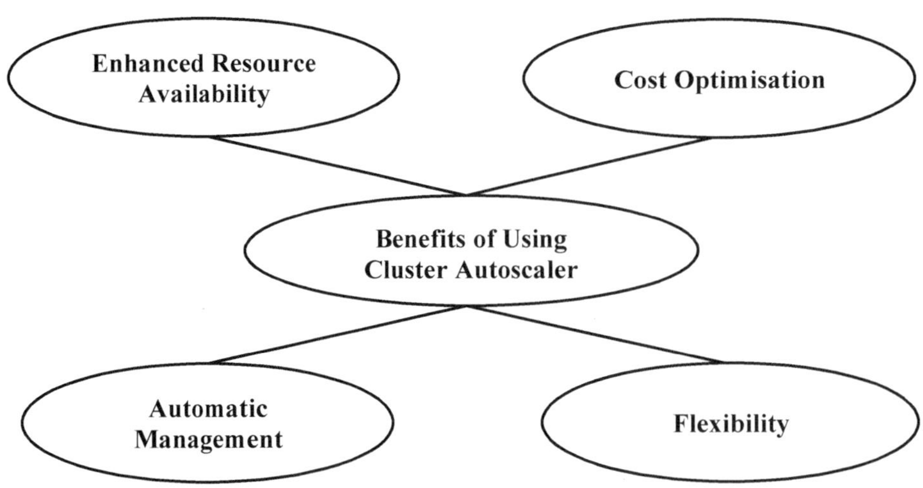

Benefits of Using Cluster Autoscaler
Enhanced Resource Availability: Ensures workloads always have enough capacity to run, even during peak usage.
Cost Optimisation: Reduces costs by terminating idle nodes and scaling down underutilised resources.
Automatic Management: Simplifies infrastructure management by automating node provisioning and de-provisioning.
Flexibility: Supports a wide range of cloud providers and custom configurations.

Challenges and Considerations
Despite its advantages, the Cluster Autoscaler has some limitations:
Scaling Delays: Provisioning new nodes can take time, potentially impacting performance during sudden workload spikes.
Cloud Provider Dependency: The autoscaler's functionality depends on the underlying cloud provider's APIs and capabilities.
Complexity: Proper configuration requires understanding both Kubernetes and the cloud provider's autoscaling options.

The Cluster Autoscaler is an essential tool for maintaining a balance between resource availability and cost-efficiency in Kubernetes environments. By dynamically adjusting the cluster's size, it ensures optimal performance and efficient use of infrastructure.

9.4 Summary
HPA: Scales the number of pods dynamically based on resource utilization metrics (e.g., CPU, memory), optimising performance and cost.
VPA: Adjusts CPU and memory requests/limits for individual pods, ensuring efficient resource allocation.
Cluster Autoscaler: Manages scaling of cluster worker nodes, adding or removing nodes to match workload demands.
Benefits: Improved application performance, cost savings, and simplified management across all autoscalers.
Challenges: Dependence on metrics/server configurations, scaling latency, and potential resource conflicts between autoscalers.

9.5 Glossary
HPA (Horizontal Pod Autoscaler): Automatically adjusts pod counts based on metrics like CPU or memory usage.
VPA (Vertical Pod Autoscaler): Optimizes pod resources (CPU, memory) by adjusting their allocation dynamically.
Cluster Autoscaler: Scales the number of nodes in a Kubernetes cluster to meet workload demands.
Resource Requests and Limits: Configurations that define the minimum and maximum resources a pod can use.
Eviction: Restarting pods to apply updated resource allocations or configurations.

Exercise

Exercise 1 - Choose the correct answer from the given options.

1. What is the primary purpose of the Horizontal Pod Autoscaler (HPA) in Kubernetes?
  a) To automatically adjust the CPU and memory limits of Pods
  b) To scale the number of Pods based on observed metrics
  c) To scale the number of Nodes in the cluster
  d) To scale the Kubernetes control plane

2. Which metric is commonly used by the Horizontal Pod Autoscaler (HPA) to determine scaling?
a) Disk I/O
b) Memory usage
c) CPU utilisation
d) Network bandwidth

Exercise 2 - Check if the sentence is true or false.

1. The Horizontal Pod Autoscaler (HPA) automatically adjusts the number of pod replicas based on CPU or memory usage.

2. The Vertical Pod Autoscaler (VPA) adjusts the number of replicas of pods based on resource usage.

Exercise 3 - Answer the following questions in your own words.

1. What automatically adjusts the number of pods based on load?

2. What adjusts the resources allocated to a pod based on its usage?

Exercise 4 - Fill the blank space with the correct word.

1. The ________ automatically scales the number of pods in a deployment based on observed CPU utilisation or other selected metrics.

2. The ________ adjusts the resources (CPU and memory) assigned to individual pods based on usage patterns.

Exercise 5 - Match each word or phrase in Column A with Column B

1. Horizontal Pod Autoscaler (HPA)
2. Vertical Pod Autoscaler (VPA)
3. Cluster Autoscaling
4. Scaling Thresholds
5. Autoscaling Policies

a) Adds or removes nodes in the cluster based on resource demands.
b) Adjusts the number of Pods based on CPU or memory usage.
c) Adjusts the resource requests and limits for existing Pods.
d) Specifies rules for when and how scaling actions are performed.
e) Defines the resource usage level that triggers scaling.

Exercise 6 - The following questions consist of two statements: Assertion (A) and Reason (R). Answer these questions, selecting the appropriate options given below:

1. Assertion (A): Horizontal Pod Autoscaler (HPA) automatically scales the number of pod replicas based on observed CPU utilisation or custom metrics.

Reason (R): HPA is responsible for adjusting the pod's CPU and memory allocation, but not the number of pod replicas.

Alternatives:

a) Assertion (A) is true, and Reason (R) is the correct reason for Assertion (A).
b) Assertion (A) is true, but Reason (R) is not the correct reason for Assertion (A).
c) Assertion (A) is false, but Reason (R) is true.
d) Assertion (A) is true, but Reason (R) is false.

2. Assertion (A): Vertical Pod Autoscaler (VPA) automatically adjusts the CPU and memory resource requests and limits for pods based on observed usage.

Reason (R): VPA increases the number of pod replicas to accommodate resource spikes, ensuring the pod's availability.

Alternatives:

a) Assertion (A) is true, and Reason (R) is the correct reason for Assertion (A).
b) Assertion (A) is true, but Reason (R) is not the correct reason for Assertion (A).
c) Assertion (A) is false, but Reason (R) is true.
d) Assertion (A) is true, but Reason (R) is false.

Exercise 7 - Answer the following questions in 50 - 80 words.

1. What is the purpose of autoscaling in Kubernetes?
2. How does the Horizontal Pod Autoscaler (HPA) work in Kubernetes?

Exercise 8 - Answer the following questions in 100 - 120 words.

1. What is Horizontal Pod Autoscaling (HPA) in Kubernetes, and how does it automatically scale the number of Pods based on resource usage like CPU and memory?
2. Explain the process of setting up a Horizontal Pod Autoscaler in Kubernetes. What metrics does it use to determine when to scale Pods up or down?

Answer

Exercise 1 - 1 b), 2 c).
Exercise 2 - 1 True, 2 False.
Exercise 3 - 1 HPA, 2 VPA.
Exercise 4 - 1 Horizontal Pod Autoscaler (HPA), 2 Vertical Pod Autoscaler (VPA).
Exercise 5 - 1 b), 2 c), 3 a), 4 e), 5 d).
Exercise 6 - 1 b), 2 d).

Online Resources

Online Exam Paper: https://forms.gle/RoDKewq4B1yNKgu49

QR Code:

Chapter 10 - Scheduling

Learning Objectives

Understand the basics of Kubernetes scheduling and how Pods are assigned to nodes.
Learn how to use taints and tolerations to control Pod placement on specific nodes.
Explore topology spread constraints to ensure even distribution of Pods across cluster nodes.
Understand how Pod priorities influence scheduling decisions and manage resource contention.
Gain knowledge about Pod evictions and how they are triggered to maintain cluster stability.

10.1 Basics

Scheduling is a fundamental concept in computer science and operations research that refers to the allocation of resources over time to accomplish a set of tasks. The primary objective of scheduling is to optimise one or more performance criteria, such as minimizing the total time to complete all tasks (makespan), maximizing resource utilisation, or meeting deadlines for time-sensitive tasks. Scheduling is ubiquitous and finds applications in various domains, including operating systems, manufacturing, project management, and cloud computing.

In the context of operating systems, scheduling primarily involves managing the execution of processes on the CPU and other system resources. The operating system's scheduler is responsible for determining which process should execute at any given time, based on specific scheduling algorithms. These algorithms are designed to ensure fairness, efficiency, and responsiveness, balancing the needs of all processes while adhering to system constraints.

There are two main types of scheduling: preemptive and non-preemptive. Preemptive scheduling allows the operating system to interrupt a running process to assign the CPU to another process, enabling a more dynamic and responsive system. Non-preemptive scheduling, on the other hand, ensures that a process runs to completion once it starts, which simplifies management but may lead to inefficiencies, such as longer wait times for certain tasks.

Scheduling in the manufacturing domain involves assigning tasks to machines or workers to optimise production efficiency. The goal may be to minimize delays, reduce costs, or ensure the timely delivery of products. Techniques like Gantt charts, priority rules, and heuristic algorithms are often employed to manage scheduling challenges in this context.

In project management, scheduling entails creating a timeline for tasks and resource allocation to achieve project milestones and deliverables. Tools like Critical Path Method (CPM) and Program Evaluation and Review Technique (PERT) are commonly used to plan and monitor project schedules, accounting for task dependencies and uncertainties.

Cloud computing has introduced new dimensions to scheduling, where the focus is on allocating virtual resources to applications dynamically. Scheduling in cloud environments aims to optimise resource utilisation while meeting service-level agreements (SLAs) for performance and cost efficiency. Algorithms in this space often leverage machine learning and predictive analytics to handle the complexity of modern cloud workloads.

Despite its wide-ranging applications, scheduling is inherently a challenging problem due to its computational complexity. Many scheduling problems are classified as NP-hard, which means that finding an optimal solution in a reasonable amount of time is often impractical. As a result, heuristic and approximation algorithms are widely used to find near-optimal solutions in real-world scenarios.

Understanding the basics of scheduling lays the groundwork for exploring advanced topics, such as multi-core scheduling, real-time scheduling, and distributed scheduling. Each of these areas introduces unique challenges and requires specialised techniques to achieve desired outcomes. By mastering scheduling concepts, one can design systems and processes that are more efficient, reliable, and responsive to dynamic demands.

10.2 Taints and tolerations

Taints and tolerations are mechanisms in Kubernetes that influence pod scheduling decisions by ensuring that certain workloads are placed on or avoided by specific nodes. These features provide a powerful way to control resource utilisation and maintain workload isolation in a Kubernetes cluster.

A taint is a label applied to a node that prevents pods from being scheduled on it unless they explicitly tolerate the taint. Taints are key-value pairs with an associated effect, which defines the consequence if a pod does not tolerate the taint. The three possible effects are:

NoSchedule: Pods that do not tolerate this taint will not be scheduled on the node.

PreferNoSchedule: Pods that do not tolerate this taint are less likely to be scheduled on the node, but scheduling is not strictly prohibited.

NoExecute: Existing pods that do not tolerate this taint are evicted from the node, and new pods will not be scheduled on it.

Tolerations, on the other hand, are specifications applied to pods that allow them to be scheduled on nodes with matching taints. Toleration specifies the key, value, and effect of the taint it tolerates, enabling fine-grained control over pod placement. This mechanism is particularly useful for use cases like dedicating nodes for specific workloads, isolating critical applications, or managing heterogeneous environments with specialised hardware.

For example, a node might be tainted with a key-value pair such as key=high-priority: NoSchedule to indicate that only high-priority workloads are allowed. Pods intended for such nodes would include a corresponding toleration in their specifications, ensuring they can be scheduled appropriately.

By combining taints and tolerations, cluster administrators can implement advanced scheduling policies that enhance the reliability, performance, and security of their Kubernetes clusters. This approach also simplifies the management of diverse workloads, as it enforces rules at the node level while allowing flexibility at the pod level.

Understanding taints and tolerations is essential for effective Kubernetes scheduling. These mechanisms not only enable better resource management but also contribute to maintaining a stable and predictable cluster environment, even under dynamic and high-demand conditions.

10.3 Topology spread Constraints

Topology spread constraints are an advanced Kubernetes feature that ensures pods are distributed evenly across the available topology domains, such as zones, nodes, or racks. This mechanism helps improve fault tolerance, minimize resource contention, and enhance workload resiliency by avoiding overloading specific parts of the infrastructure.

A topology spread constraint specifies the desired distribution of pods across a particular topology domain. For instance, a developer might require that a deployment's pods be evenly spread across multiple availability zones to mitigate the impact of zone failures. Kubernetes enforces these constraints during scheduling, attempting to place pods in a way that meets the specified distribution requirements.

Each topology spread constraint is defined using the following key parameters:

Topology Key: Represents the node label that defines the topology domain, such as topology.kubernetes.io/zone or kubernetes.io/hostname.

Max Skew: Indicates the maximum allowable difference in the number of pods between the most and least loaded topology domains.

When Unsatisfiable: Determines the scheduler's behaviour when the constraint cannot be satisfied. The two options are:

- **DoNotSchedule**: Prevents scheduling new pods if it would violate the constraint.
- **ScheduleAnyway**: Allows scheduling even if the constraint is violated but prioritises adherence.

Label Selector: Filters the set of pods to which the constraint applies based on their labels.

Organisations can ensure high availability and balanced resource usage by leveraging topology spread constraints. For example, a stateful application might use this feature to distribute its replicas across zones, ensuring continued availability even if one zone experiences an outage. Similarly, batch jobs can be spread across nodes to optimise resource utilisation and prevent contention.

However, topology spread constraints do not guarantee perfect distribution, as they depend on the cluster's current state and available resources. In scenarios where the constraints cannot be satisfied, developers may need to adjust the parameters or rethink their deployment strategies to achieve the desired outcomes.

Understanding and applying topology spread constraints is critical for building robust and scalable Kubernetes workloads. This feature empowers developers and administrators to design clusters that are resilient to failures, efficient in resource usage, and capable of supporting diverse application requirements.

10.4 Pod priorities

Pod priorities are an integral feature in Kubernetes that determine the order in which pods are scheduled when resources are limited. They provide a way to prioritise critical workloads over less important ones, ensuring that essential applications continue to run even under resource constraints.

A pod's priority is defined using the PriorityClass object, which assigns a numerical value to represent the pod's importance. Higher numerical values indicate higher priority. Kubernetes uses this priority value during scheduling to decide which pods should preempt others if necessary.

The preemption process occurs when a high-priority pod cannot be scheduled due to insufficient resources. In such cases, the scheduler identifies and evicts lower-priority pods from their nodes to make room for the higher-priority pod. However, preemption is performed cautiously to minimize disruptions and maintain overall cluster stability.

Common use cases for pod priorities include:

Ensuring Critical Workloads Run: Assigning higher priorities to critical system components or business applications ensures they remain operational during resource shortages.

Graceful Degradation: Lowering the priority of less critical workloads allows them to be preempted first, enabling essential applications to continue functioning.

Batch Processing: Assigning low priorities to batch jobs ensures they do not interfere with real-time or interactive applications.

To define a priority class, administrators create a **PriorityClass** object with a name, a numerical value, and an optional description. For example:

```
apiVersion: scheduling.k8s.io/v1
kind: PriorityClass
metadata:
  name: high-priority
value: 1000
globalDefault: false
description: "This priority class is for high-priority workloads."
```

Pods can then reference this priority class in their specifications to inherit the defined priority. By carefully managing pod priorities, organisations can ensure optimal resource allocation and maintain application performance during high-demand periods.

It is important to note that misuse of pod priorities can lead to resource starvation for low-priority workloads or excessive preemptions, destabilising the cluster. Therefore, administrators must design and implement priority schemes thoughtfully, considering the needs of all applications and the overall cluster environment.

10.5 Evictions

Evictions in Kubernetes refer to the process of removing a pod from its node, often to ensure optimal resource utilisation, maintain cluster stability, or comply with scheduling policies. Evictions can occur for various reasons, including resource shortages, node maintenance, or adherence to quality of service (QoS) guarantees.

There are two primary types of evictions in Kubernetes:
Soft Evictions: These occur when the system proactively evicts pods based on resource thresholds defined by the administrator. For instance, if a node's memory or CPU usage exceeds a predefined limit, Kubernetes may evict less critical pods to free up resources. Soft evictions allow workloads to adapt gracefully to resource constraints and are governed by parameters like evictionHard and evictionSoft in the Kubernetes configuration.
Hard Evictions: These are immediate and non-negotiable evictions triggered by critical events, such as node failures or system errors. Hard evictions prioritise maintaining cluster integrity and may result in the abrupt termination of pods.

Evictions also play a crucial role in enforcing QoS guarantees. Pods in Kubernetes are categorised into three QoS **classes:** Guaranteed, Burstable, and BestEffort. When evictions are necessary, pods in the BestEffort class are evicted first, followed by Burstable pods, while Guaranteed pods are typically the last to be evicted. This hierarchy ensures that critical workloads with higher QoS guarantees are prioritised during resource shortages.
Administrators can configure eviction behaviours using policies such as PodDisruptionBudgets (PDBs). PDBs define the minimum number or percentage of replicas that must remain available during voluntary disruptions, such as evictions caused by node maintenance or cluster upgrades. By setting appropriate PDBs, organisations can minimize downtime and maintain application availability during planned disruptions.
It is essential to monitor and manage evictions carefully to prevent unintended consequences, such as application downtime or cascading failures. Tools like Kubernetes events, metrics, and logging systems provide insights into eviction activities, enabling administrators to identify and address potential issues proactively.
By understanding and leveraging eviction mechanisms, organisations can build resilient and adaptable Kubernetes clusters that maintain performance and stability under dynamic conditions.

10.6 Summary

Scheduling Basics: Involves allocating resources over time to optimize performance criteria like efficiency, resource utilization, or deadlines, and is applied in domains like OS, manufacturing, and cloud computing.
Taints and Tolerations: Taints prevent pods from being scheduled on nodes without explicit tolerations, enabling workload isolation and resource management.
Topology Spread Constraints: Distributes pods across topology domains (zones, nodes) to ensure fault tolerance and balanced resource usage.
Pod Priorities: Assign importance levels to pods, prioritising critical workloads during scheduling and preempting lower-priority pods if resources are limited.
Evictions: Removes pods from nodes to maintain resource availability or enforce policies, with QoS guarantees determining eviction order to minimize disruptions.

10.7 Glossary

Scheduling: Allocation of tasks or resources over time to meet performance objectives in various domains.
Taint: A node-level label that prevents unscheduled pods unless tolerations are defined.
Topology Spread Constraints: Ensures pod distribution across specific infrastructure domains to enhance resiliency.
Pod Priority: A numerical value indicating the scheduling importance of a pod.
Eviction: The process of removing pods from nodes due to resource shortages or policy adherence.

Exercise

Exercise 1 - Choose the correct answer from the given options.

1. What is the primary role of the Kubernetes scheduler?

a) To manage container networking

b) To assign Pods to appropriate Nodes in the cluster

c) To monitor the health of Pods

d) To configure resource quotas for Pods

2. What is the purpose of Taints in Kubernetes scheduling?

a) To set resource limits for Pods

b) To prevent Pods from being scheduled on certain Nodes unless they tolerate the taint

c) To control the networking between Pods

d) To define the priority of Pods

Exercise 2 - Check if the sentence is true or false.

1. Scheduling in Kubernetes determines how and where pods are placed within a cluster.

2. Taints in Kubernetes are used to prevent pods from being scheduled on certain nodes unless the pod has a matching toleration.

Exercise 3 - Answer the following questions in your own words.

1. What defines the basic principles of scheduling in Kubernetes?

2. What is used to control which pods can be scheduled on specific nodes?

Exercise 4 - Fill the blank space with the correct word.

1. Kubernetes uses a ________ to assign pods to nodes based on resource availability and other constraints.

2. ________ allow you to mark nodes so that only pods with matching tolerations can be scheduled onto those nodes.

Exercise 5 - Match each word or phrase in Column A with Column B

1. Basics
2. Taints and tolerations
3. Topology spread constraints
4. Pod priorities
5. Evictions

a) Controls which Pods can or cannot be scheduled on specific nodes.

b) Removes Pods from a node to free resources or due to constraints.

c) Fundamental concepts of assigning Pods to nodes.

d) Ensures even distribution of Pods across failure domains like zones.

e) Determines the importance of Pods during resource contention.

Exercise 6 - The following questions consist of two statements: Assertion (A) and Reason (R). Answer these questions, selecting the appropriate options given below:

1. Assertion (A): Taints and tolerations in Kubernetes are used to control the scheduling of pods onto nodes based on specific conditions.

Reason (R): Taints prevent pods from being scheduled on nodes, but tolerations allow pods to be scheduled on those nodes even with the taint.

Alternatives:

a) Assertion (A) is true, and Reason (R) is the correct reason for Assertion (A).
b) Assertion (A) is true, but Reason (R) is not the correct reason for Assertion (A).
c) Assertion (A) is false, but Reason (R) is true.
d) Assertion (A) is true, but Reason (R) is false.

2. Assertion (A): Topology spread constraints ensure that Kubernetes pods are evenly distributed across different failure domains, such as zones or regions.

Reason (R): Topology spread constraints can only control the distribution of pods across nodes in the same zone, not across multiple zones or regions.

Alternatives:

a) Assertion (A) is true, and Reason (R) is the correct reason for Assertion (A).
b) Assertion (A) is true, but Reason (R) is not the correct reason for Assertion (A).
c) Assertion (A) is false, but Reason (R) is true.
d) Assertion (A) is true, but Reason (R) is false.

Exercise 7 - Answer the following questions in 50 - 80 words.

1. What is the primary purpose of scheduling in Kubernetes?
2. How does Kubernetes decide which node to assign a Pod to?

Exercise 8 - Answer the following questions in 100 - 120 words.

1. What is the role of the Kubernetes scheduler, and how does it decide where to place Pods within a cluster? Explain the basic principles of scheduling in Kubernetes.

2. What are the key factors the Kubernetes scheduler considers when determining the best node for running a Pod? How do resource requirements, affinity rules, and taints impact the scheduling decisions?

Answer

Exercise 1 - 1 b), 2 b).
Exercise 2 - 1 True, 2 True.
Exercise 3 - 1 Basics, 2 Taints.
Exercise 4 - 1 Scheduler, 2 Taints.
Exercise 5 - 1 c), 2 a), 3 d), 4 e), 5 b).
Exercise 6 - 1 a), 2 d).

Online Resources

Online Exam Paper: https://forms.gle/CjAi7ouo2rC3iRJh8

QR Code:

Chapter 11 - Storage and Volumes

Learning Objectives

Understand the role of CSI (Container Storage Interface) drivers in managing storage across diverse environments in Kubernetes.

Learn how to configure and use persistent storage solutions for stateful applications in Kubernetes.

Explore best practices for managing storage requirements for applications with persistent data needs.

Gain insights into the integration of storage systems with Kubernetes for efficient data management.

Understand how storage and volumes impact the deployment and scaling of stateful applications.

11.1 CSI Drivers

The Container Storage Interface (CSI) is a standardised interface that allows storage vendors to develop plugins for their storage solutions that work seamlessly with container orchestration platforms like Kubernetes. CSI drivers act as the bridge between container orchestrators and the underlying storage systems, enabling developers and operators to manage storage resources consistently and efficiently.

What are CSI Drivers?

CSI drivers are external plugins implemented by storage vendors to expose storage functionality to containerised applications. They standardise how storage operations such as provisioning, attaching, mounting, and snapshotting are performed, irrespective of the underlying storage infrastructure. This abstraction simplifies the integration of various storage solutions with Kubernetes and other orchestrators that support CSI.

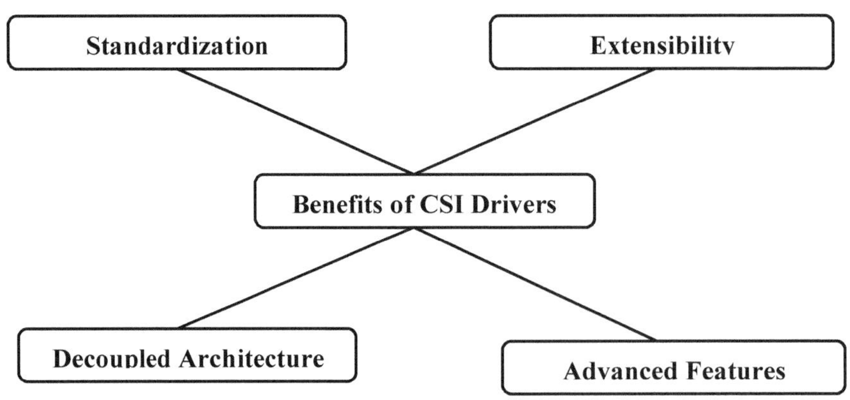

Benefits of CSI Drivers

Standardization: CSI drivers provide a consistent interface for storage operations, reducing the complexity of managing diverse storage systems.

Extensibility: They enable support for a wide range of storage backends, including block storage, file systems, and cloud-native storage solutions.

Decoupled Architecture: By externalising storage drivers, CSI decouples storage logic from Kubernetes core components, allowing independent updates and enhancements.

Advanced Features: Many CSI drivers support advanced storage features such as snapshots, clones, and volume expansion, enhancing application resilience and flexibility.

How CSI Drivers Work

CSI drivers interact with the container orchestration platform through a set of defined APIs. These APIs enable communication for essential storage operations such as:

Provisioning: Creating new storage volumes dynamically based on user-defined specifications.
Attachment: Connecting a storage volume to a specific node for use by a pod.
Mounting: Making the volume accessible within a pod's filesystem.
Snapshotting: Capturing point-in-time snapshots of storage volumes for backup and recovery.
Expansion: Resizing storage volumes to meet growing application needs.
The Kubernetes CSI implementation relies on custom resources such as StorageClass, PersistentVolume, and PersistentVolumeClaim to define and manage storage requirements. The CSI driver fulfills these requirements by communicating with the backend storage system through the CSI APIs.

Deployment and Configuration
Deploying a CSI driver in Kubernetes involves:
Driver Installation: Installing the CSI driver as a set of pods (often using a Helm chart or YAML manifests) in the Kubernetes cluster.
StorageClass Definition: Creating a StorageClass object to define the storage attributes and policies for dynamic provisioning.
Persistent Volume Claims: Users create PersistentVolumeClaim objects, which are automatically fulfilled by the CSI driver using the specified StorageClass.
Pod Integration: Attaching the claimed storage volumes to pods through the volume specification in the pod manifest.

Examples of Popular CSI Drivers
AWS EBS CSI Driver: Integrates Amazon Elastic Block Store with Kubernetes.
Azure Disk CSI Driver: Provides support for Azure-managed disks.
Google PD CSI Driver: Enables Kubernetes integration with Google Persistent Disks.
Ceph CSI Driver: Supports Ceph RBD and CephFS for scalable block and file storage.
OpenEBS CSI Driver: Offers container-attached storage solutions for Kubernetes.

CSI drivers have revolutionised how storage is managed in containerised environments by abstracting the complexities of underlying storage systems. They enable Kubernetes to support a vast ecosystem of storage solutions, ensuring scalability, portability, and ease of management. As storage technologies evolve, CSI drivers will continue to play a crucial role in bridging the gap between advanced storage capabilities and containerised workloads.

11.2 Stateful Applications

Stateful applications are software systems that maintain persistent data across multiple sessions or interactions. Unlike stateless applications, where the state is not preserved between requests, stateful applications require a storage backend to save data and ensure continuity. Examples of stateful applications include databases, message queues, and caching systems.

Importance of Stateful Applications
Stateful applications are critical for modern workloads that need data integrity and persistence. These applications often manage vital business operations such as transaction processing, user session management, and real-time data analytics. Ensuring proper storage and management of data for stateful applications is essential for maintaining high availability, reliability, and performance.

Challenges of Managing Stateful Applications in Kubernetes
Managing stateful applications in containerised environments like Kubernetes poses unique challenges, including:

Persistent Storage: Unlike ephemeral storage, which is lost when a container restarts, stateful applications need storage that persists across container and pod lifecycles.

Data Consistency: Ensuring data consistency when pods are rescheduled or scaled.

Pod Affinity: Stateful applications often require specific pods to access the same storage volumes, which necessitates careful scheduling.

Scaling: Scaling stateful applications is more complex than stateless ones, as it involves maintaining a consistent state across replicas.

Kubernetes Solutions for Stateful Applications

Kubernetes provides several mechanisms to address the challenges of running stateful applications:

StatefulSets:

Kubernetes offers StatefulSets as a controller specifically designed for managing stateful applications. It ensures stable pod identities, ordered deployment, and persistent storage association.

Pods managed by a StatefulSet are assigned a unique identifier that allows them to retain their network and storage configurations.

Persistent Volumes (PVs) and Persistent Volume Claims (PVCs):

Kubernetes' PersistentVolume (PV) and PersistentVolumeClaim (PVC) abstractions decouple storage provisioning from pod management.

These resources ensure that stateful applications have access to reliable and persistent storage.

StorageClass:

StorageClasses define the parameters for dynamic storage provisioning. Different types of storage (e.g., SSD, HDD, cloud-native storage) can be specified to suit application requirements.

Volume Affinity:

Kubernetes supports volume affinity policies to ensure that pods are scheduled on nodes where their associated storage is available, reducing latency and improving reliability.

Snapshots and Backups:

CSI drivers often enable snapshotting functionality, allowing administrators to take point-in-time snapshots of application data for backup and recovery.

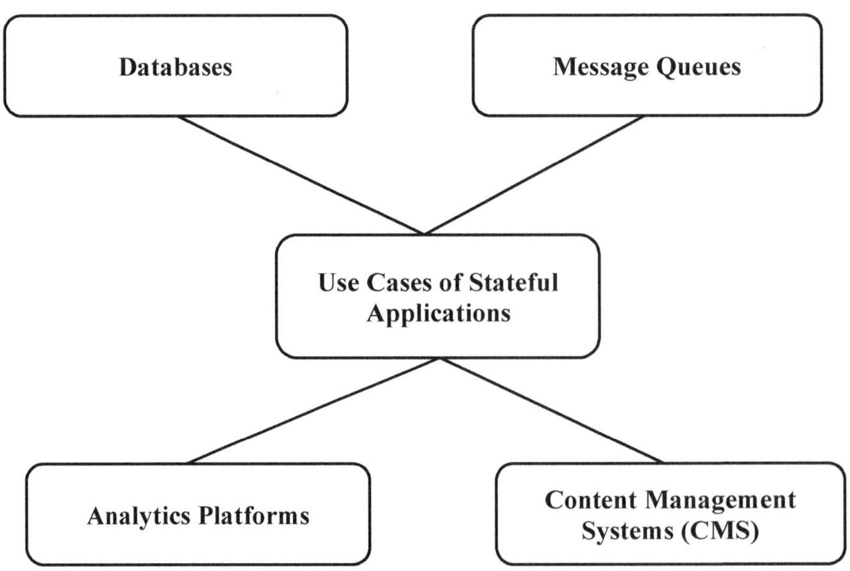

Common Use Cases of Stateful Applications

Databases: Applications such as MySQL, PostgreSQL, MongoDB, and Cassandra require persistent storage for maintaining data integrity and ensuring transactional consistency.
Message Queues: Systems like RabbitMQ and Kafka rely on state to manage messaging sequences and acknowledgments.
Analytics Platforms: Real-time analytics tools like Elasticsearch and Prometheus require stateful storage for indexing and querying historical data.
Content Management Systems (CMS): CMS platforms such as WordPress and Drupal store user-generated content and metadata in persistent storage.

Best Practices for Running Stateful Applications in Kubernetes
Use StatefulSets: Leverage StatefulSets for predictable pod identities and stable storage attachments.
Plan Storage Requirements: Analyse application needs to choose appropriate storage classes and capacity.
Implement Backup Strategies: Use snapshots and replication for disaster recovery and fault tolerance.
Monitor Performance: Use monitoring tools to ensure storage and application performance meet operational requirements.
Automate with Operators: Employ Kubernetes operators to automate the deployment, scaling, and maintenance of complex stateful applications.

Stateful applications are integral to many critical workloads and require specialised handling in containerised environments. Kubernetes provides robust constructs like StatefulSets, PersistentVolumes, and StorageClasses to support the unique needs of stateful workloads. By understanding and leveraging these features, organisations can ensure their stateful applications run efficiently and reliably in Kubernetes.

11.3 Summary
CSI Drivers: Standardize storage management in Kubernetes, supporting various storage backends like block storage and cloud-native solutions.
Benefits of CSI: Provide consistent interfaces, extensibility, decoupled architecture, and advanced features such as snapshots.
How It Works: CSI drivers interact with Kubernetes APIs for storage provisioning, attachment, mounting, and expansion.
Stateful Applications: Require persistent storage for maintaining data integrity across multiple sessions, such as databases and message queues.
Kubernetes Solutions for Stateful Applications: Use StatefulSets, PersistentVolumes, and StorageClasses for reliable storage management.
Best Practices: Use StatefulSets, plan storage needs, and implement backup strategies for stateful workloads.

11.4 Glossary
CSI Driver: A plugin developed by storage vendors to manage storage operations in Kubernetes through a standard interface.
Stateful Application: Applications that require persistent data storage across sessions, like databases or analytics tools.
StatefulSet: A Kubernetes controller designed to manage stateful applications with stable pod identities and persistent storage.
Persistent Volume (PV): A Kubernetes resource that represents storage provisioned for pod use.
StorageClass: A Kubernetes object that defines parameters for dynamic storage provisioning, such as type and performance.
Snapshot: A point-in-time backup of a storage volume, often used for data recovery.

Exercise

Exercise 1 - Choose the correct answer from the given options.

1. What does the Container Storage Interface (CSI) in Kubernetes enable?

a) It enables container networking

b) It enables the dynamic provisioning of storage resources

c) It enables the management of container logs

d) It enables the monitoring and scaling of Pods

2. Which of the following is a key feature of CSI drivers in Kubernetes?

a) They allow Pods to communicate with other Pods

b) They handle the configuration of Kubernetes namespaces

c) They provide a standardised interface for storage plugins

d) They control the scaling of deployments

Exercise 2 - Check if the sentence is true or false.

1. CSI (Container Storage Interface) drivers enable Kubernetes to interact with different storage systems.

2. Stateful applications in Kubernetes require persistent storage to retain their data across pod restarts.

Exercise 3 - Answer the following questions in your own words.

1. What is used to integrate storage solutions with Kubernetes?

2. What type of drivers provide storage for Kubernetes?

Exercise 4 - Fill the blank space with the correct word.

1. ________ enable Kubernetes to use different storage systems and integrate with external storage providers.

2. ________ in Kubernetes are responsible for abstracting storage resources and providing a consistent interface for applications.

Exercise 5 - Match each word or phrase in Column A with Column B

1. CSI Drivers
2. Stateful Applications
3. Persistent Volumes (PV)
4. Persistent Volume Claims
5. Dynamic Provisioning

a) Allocates storage that Pods can use.

b) Automatically provisions storage based on user requests.

c) Provides a standardised interface for storage plugins in Kubernetes.

d) Requires persistent storage to maintain data consistency.

e) Allows users to request specific storage resources.

Exercise 6 - The following questions consist of two statements: Assertion (A) and Reason (R). Answer these questions, selecting the appropriate options given below:

1. Assertion (A): CSI (Container Storage Interface) drivers allow Kubernetes to interact with various storage solutions.

Reason (R): CSI drivers are responsible for scheduling pods across multiple nodes in a Kubernetes cluster.

Alternatives:

a) Assertion (A) is true, and Reason (R) is the correct reason for Assertion (A).
b) Assertion (A) is true, but Reason (R) is not the correct reason for Assertion (A).
c) Assertion (A) is false, but Reason (R) is true.
d) Assertion (A) is true, but Reason (R) is false.

2. Assertion (A): Stateful applications in Kubernetes require persistent storage to maintain data across pod restarts.
Reason (R): Stateful applications rely on Kubernetes ConfigMaps to store persistent data.
Alternatives:
a) Assertion (A) is true, and Reason (R) is the correct reason for Assertion (A).
b) Assertion (A) is true, but Reason (R) is not the correct reason for Assertion (A).
c) Assertion (A) is false, but Reason (R) is true.
d) Assertion (A) is true, but Reason (R) is false.

Exercise 7 - Answer the following questions in 50 - 80 words.
1. What is the role of storage in Kubernetes?
2. What are Kubernetes volumes, and how are they used?

Exercise 8 - Answer the following questions in 100 - 120 words.
1. What are CSI (Container Storage Interface) drivers in Kubernetes, and how do they standardise the process of integrating storage solutions with Kubernetes clusters?
2. Explain the role of CSI drivers in managing dynamic storage provisioning. How do they simplify storage operations in a Kubernetes environment?

Answer

Exercise 1 - 1 b), 2 c).
Exercise 2 - 1 True, 2 True.
Exercise 3 - 1 CSI, 2 CSI.
Exercise 4 - 1 CSI Drivers, 2 Volumes.
Exercise 5 - 1 c), 2 d), 3 a), 4 e), 5 b).
Exercise 6 - 1 d), 2 b).

Online Resources

Online Exam Paper: https://forms.gle/BDGqHMCFt5zVoNgs6

QR Code:

Chapter 12 - Sample Question Paper

General Instructions:
Time Allowed: 3 Hours
Maximum Marks: 100
Answer all the questions.
Marks are indicated against each question.

SECTION-A

I. Multiple Choice Questions **(2x5=10 Marks)**

1. Which of the following is a Kubernetes controller responsible for maintaining a specified number of pod replicas?
a) Pod
b) ReplicaSet
c) StatefulSet
d) Service

2. What is the primary purpose of ConfigMaps in Kubernetes?
a) Storing sensitive data securely
b) Managing container networking
c) Injecting configuration into pods
d) Monitoring resource usage

3. Which Kubernetes resource is used for running long-running, fault-tolerant services?
a) Job
b) Pod
c) Deployment
d) CronJob

4. How does Horizontal Pod Autoscaler (HPA) scale workloads in Kubernetes?
a) Adding CPU cores to existing pods
b) Adjusting pod memory limits
c) Increasing or decreasing the number of pods
d) Scheduling pods on specific nodes

5. What is the role of RBAC in Kubernetes?
a) Providing persistent storage
b) Managing access control to resources
c) Handling pod networking
d) Scheduling pods across nodes

SECTION-B

II. Fill in the Blanks **(2x5=10 Marks)**

1. __________ is used to expose a Kubernetes service to the external network.
2. The __________ ensures no single node is overwhelmed by traffic.
3. __________ allows secure storage of sensitive information like API keys and passwords in Kubernetes.
4. __________ constraints help distribute pods evenly across zones or racks.
5. The __________ manages the lifecycle of volumes used by StatefulSets.

SECTION-C

III. Very Short Answer Type Questions-I **(4x5=20 Marks)**

1. Define Kubernetes and explain its primary purpose.
2. Explain the concept of a StatefulSet and its use cases.
3. What are taints and tolerations in Kubernetes, and why are they used?
4. List two benefits of using managed Kubernetes providers.

IV. Short Answer Type Questions-II **(6x5=30 Marks)**

1. Differentiate between ConfigMaps and Secrets in Kubernetes.
2. Explain the significance of resource requests and limits in optimising application performance.
3. What is the function of the Vertical Pod Autoscaler (VPA)?
4. Discuss the importance of monitoring logs and metrics in Kubernetes.
5. Describe the steps involved in setting up role-based access control (RBAC).

SECTION-D

V. Long Answer Type Questions **(10x3=30 Marks)**

1. Discuss the Kubernetes networking model, including pod-to-pod communication and external access to services.
2. Describe the steps to deploy a StatefulSet in Kubernetes and the considerations for persistent storage.
3. Explain the importance of Cluster Autoscaling and how it handles varying workloads.

Chapter 13 – Certification Questions

1. What is the primary purpose of a Network Policy in Kubernetes?
A. Monitoring network traffic
B. Managing Pod-to-Pod communication within the cluster
C. Assigning roles and permissions
D. Balancing traffic between nodes
Answer: B

2. Which command is used to view the logs of a Pod?
A. kubectl exec
B. kubectl describe
C. kubectl logs
D. kubectl get logs
Answer: C

3. What does Cluster Autoscaler do when it identifies underutilized nodes?
A. Deletes the nodes
B. Automatically increases Pod replicas
C. Scales down the cluster by removing unused nodes
D. Reschedules Pods onto new nodes
Answer: C

4. Which Kubernetes feature enables storage plugins to provision volumes dynamically?
A. VolumeMount
B. StatefulSet
C. StorageClass
D. ReplicaSet
Answer: C

5. What is the smallest deployable unit in Kubernetes?
A. Deployment
B. Node
C. Pod
D. ReplicaSet
Answer: C

6. What is the purpose of a taint in Kubernetes?
A. To prioritize specific Pods for scheduling
B. To prevent Pods from being scheduled on certain nodes unless tolerated
C. To monitor the health of nodes
D. To set resource limits for Pods
Answer: B

7. What happens if a Pod exceeds its memory limit in Kubernetes?
A. The Pod runs without restrictions
B. The Node automatically adds more memory
C. The Pod is evicted
D. The Pod is throttled
Answer: C

8. Which resource is responsible for scaling Pods based on CPU or memory usage?
A. Cluster Autoscaler
B. Vertical Pod Autoscaler (VPA)
C. ReplicaSet

D. Horizontal Pod Autoscaler (HPA)
Answer: D

9. Which Kubernetes resource ensures a specified number of Pod replicas are running at all times?
A. StatefulSet
B. ReplicaSet
C. Deployment
D. Job
Answer: B

10. Which scheduling feature ensures that Pods are distributed across failure domains such as zones?
A. Tolerations
B. Topology Spread Constraints
C. Node Affinity
D. Pod Priority
Answer: B

11. What is the role of Prometheus in a Kubernetes cluster?
A. Deploying applications
B. Monitoring and collecting metrics
C. Managing container storage
D. Handling logging for applications
Answer: B

12. Which of the following tools is commonly used to create a local Kubernetes cluster?
A. Prometheus
B. Kind
C. Helm
D. Terraform
Answer: B

13. What does a Pod Security Admission (PSA) policy enforce?
A. Network access rules for Pods
B. Security configurations for Pod specifications
C. Scaling rules for Pods
D. Access control for Kubernetes resources
Answer: B

14. Which Kubernetes Service type is used to expose an application to external traffic?
A. NodePort
B. LoadBalancer
C. ExternalName
D. ClusterIP
Answer: B

15. What is the purpose of a PersistentVolume (PV) in Kubernetes?
A. To manage Pod replicas
B. To define a storage resource that can be dynamically provisioned
C. To store configuration data for Pods
D. To define network policies
Answer: B

Mastering Kubernetes: 100 Questions with Answers & Reasoning

1. What is Kubernetes?

Answer: Kubernetes is an open-source container orchestration platform.
Reasoning: It manages containerized applications by handling deployment, scaling, networking, storage, and self-healing.

2. What problem does Kubernetes solve?

Answer: It automates container management at scale.
Reasoning: Without Kubernetes, managing many containers across many servers becomes difficult and error-prone.

3. What is a Kubernetes cluster?

Answer: A group of machines running Kubernetes.
Reasoning: A cluster contains control plane nodes and worker nodes that together run applications.

4. What is the control plane?

Answer: The brain of the Kubernetes cluster.
Reasoning: It makes decisions about scheduling, scaling, and cluster state.

5. What is a worker node?

Answer: A machine where application workloads run.
Reasoning: Worker nodes host Pods, containers, kubelet, kube-proxy, and container runtime.

6. What is a Pod?

Answer: The smallest deployable unit in Kubernetes.
Reasoning: A Pod contains one or more containers that share storage and networking.

7. Why does Kubernetes use Pods instead of directly running containers?

Answer: Pods provide a higher-level abstraction.
Reasoning: They allow containers to share network, storage, and lifecycle.

8. Can a Pod contain multiple containers?

Answer: Yes.
Reasoning: Multiple containers are used when they need to work closely together, such as sidecar containers.

9. What is a sidecar container?

Answer: A helper container running with the main container in the same Pod.
Reasoning: It adds features like logging, proxying, or monitoring without changing the main application.

10. What is a Deployment?

Answer: A Kubernetes object used to manage replicated Pods.
Reasoning: Deployments provide rolling updates, rollback, and desired replica management.

11. What is a ReplicaSet?

Answer: It ensures a specified number of Pod replicas are running.
Reasoning: Deployments use ReplicaSets internally to maintain application availability.

12. What is the difference between Deployment and ReplicaSet?

Answer: Deployment manages ReplicaSets and updates.
Reasoning: ReplicaSet only maintains replicas, while Deployment supports rollout and rollback.

13. What is a StatefulSet?

Answer: A workload object for stateful applications.
Reasoning: It provides stable network identity, stable storage, and ordered deployment.

14. When should StatefulSet be used?

Answer: For databases or applications needing persistent identity.
Reasoning: Examples include MongoDB, Cassandra, and ZooKeeper.

15. What is a DaemonSet?

Answer: It runs one Pod on every selected node.
Reasoning: It is useful for logging agents, monitoring agents, or network plugins.

16. What is a Job?

Answer: A Kubernetes object that runs a task to completion.
Reasoning: Jobs are used for batch processing or one-time tasks.

17. What is a CronJob?

Answer: A scheduled Job in Kubernetes.
Reasoning: It runs tasks periodically, like backups or reports.

18. What is a Service?

Answer: A stable network endpoint for accessing Pods.
Reasoning: Pods are temporary, but Services provide a consistent way to reach them.

19. Why are Services needed?

Answer: Pod IPs can change.
Reasoning: Services abstract dynamic Pods and provide stable access.

20. What is ClusterIP?

Answer: The default Service type for internal access.
Reasoning: It exposes the Service only inside the cluster.

21. What is NodePort?

Answer: A Service type that exposes an application on each node's port.
Reasoning: It allows external traffic to reach the application through node IP and port.

22. What is LoadBalancer Service?

Answer: A Service that exposes applications using an external load balancer.
Reasoning: It is commonly used in cloud environments.

23. What is ExternalName Service?

Answer: A Service that maps to an external DNS name.
Reasoning: It allows Kubernetes applications to access external services using internal naming.

24. What is Ingress?

Answer: An API object that manages external HTTP/HTTPS access.
Reasoning: It routes traffic to Services based on hostnames or paths.

25. What is an Ingress Controller?

Answer: A component that implements Ingress rules.
Reasoning: Ingress objects need a controller like NGINX, Traefik, or HAProxy to work.

26. What is kube-apiserver?

Answer: The main entry point to the Kubernetes control plane.
Reasoning: All commands and components communicate through the API server.

27. What is etcd?

Answer: A distributed key-value store used by Kubernetes.
Reasoning: It stores cluster state and configuration.

28. Why is etcd important?

Answer: It contains the source of truth for the cluster.
Reasoning: If etcd data is lost, cluster state may be lost.

29. What is kube-scheduler?

Answer: It assigns Pods to nodes.
Reasoning: It considers resources, constraints, taints, tolerations, and affinity rules.

30. What is kube-controller-manager?

Answer: It runs controllers that maintain cluster state.
Reasoning: Controllers ensure actual state matches desired state.

31. What is kubelet?

Answer: An agent running on each worker node.
Reasoning: It ensures containers described in PodSpecs are running.

32. What is kube-proxy?

Answer: A network component that manages Service networking.
Reasoning: It handles traffic forwarding to backend Pods.

33. What is container runtime?

Answer: Software that runs containers.
Reasoning: Kubernetes needs a runtime like containerd or CRI-O to start containers.

34. What is desired state?

Answer: The state declared by the user.
Reasoning: Kubernetes continuously works to make the actual state match the desired state.

35. What is declarative configuration?

Answer: Defining what the final state should be.
Reasoning: Kubernetes YAML files describe desired resources instead of manual steps.

36. What is imperative management?

Answer: Directly issuing commands to create or modify resources.
Reasoning: Example: kubectl run creates resources immediately.

37. What is kubectl?

Answer: The command-line tool for Kubernetes.
Reasoning: It communicates with the Kubernetes API server.

38. What is a Namespace?

Answer: A logical division inside a cluster.
Reasoning: Namespaces separate resources for teams, projects, or environments.

39. Why use Namespaces?

Answer: For organization and isolation.
Reasoning: They help manage access, quotas, and resource separation.

40. What is a ConfigMap?

Answer: A Kubernetes object for storing non-sensitive configuration.
Reasoning: It separates configuration from container images.

41. What is a Secret?

Answer: An object used to store sensitive data.
Reasoning: It stores passwords, tokens, and keys more safely than plain ConfigMaps.

42. Are Kubernetes Secrets fully secure by default?

Answer: Not completely.
Reasoning: They are base64-encoded by default, not encrypted unless encryption at rest is enabled.

43. What is a Volume?

Answer: Storage attached to a Pod.
Reasoning: It allows data to persist beyond container restarts.

44. What is PersistentVolume?

Answer: A cluster storage resource.
Reasoning: It represents physical or cloud storage available to Pods.

45. What is PersistentVolumeClaim?

Answer: A request for storage by a user or application.
Reasoning: Pods use PVCs to claim PersistentVolumes.

46. What is StorageClass?

Answer: A way to define dynamic storage provisioning.
Reasoning: It allows Kubernetes to create storage automatically when PVCs are created.

47. What is dynamic provisioning?

Answer: Automatic creation of storage volumes.
Reasoning: It reduces manual storage administration.

48. What is a container image?

Answer: A packaged application with dependencies.
Reasoning: Kubernetes pulls images to run containers.

49. What is imagePullPolicy?

Answer: A setting that controls when images are pulled.
Reasoning: Common values are Always, IfNotPresent, and Never.

50. What is a readiness probe?

Answer: A check to know if a container is ready to receive traffic.
Reasoning: If readiness fails, the Pod is removed from Service endpoints.

51. What is a liveness probe?

Answer: A check to know if a container is still healthy.
Reasoning: If liveness fails, Kubernetes restarts the container.

52. What is a startup probe?

Answer: A probe used for slow-starting applications.
Reasoning: It prevents liveness probes from killing applications before they finish startup.

53. What is rolling update?

Answer: Gradually replacing old Pods with new Pods.
Reasoning: It avoids downtime during application updates.

54. What is rollback?

Answer: Returning to a previous application version.
Reasoning: It is useful when a new release fails.

55. What is scaling in Kubernetes?

Answer: Increasing or decreasing the number of Pods.
Reasoning: Scaling helps handle changing workload demand.

56. What is Horizontal Pod Autoscaler?

Answer: It automatically changes the number of Pod replicas.
Reasoning: It usually scales based on CPU, memory, or custom metrics.

57. What is Vertical Pod Autoscaler?

Answer: It adjusts CPU and memory requests for Pods.
Reasoning: It helps right-size workloads.

58. What is Cluster Autoscaler?

Answer: It adjusts the number of cluster nodes.
Reasoning: It adds nodes when Pods cannot be scheduled and removes unused nodes.

59. What are resource requests?

Answer: Minimum resources required by a container.
Reasoning: Scheduler uses requests to place Pods on nodes.

60. What are resource limits?

Answer: Maximum resources a container can use.
Reasoning: Limits prevent one container from consuming excessive resources.

61. What happens if a container exceeds memory limit?

Answer: It may be killed.
Reasoning: Kubernetes can terminate containers that exceed memory limits.

62. What happens if a container exceeds CPU limit?

Answer: It is throttled.
Reasoning: CPU usage is restricted rather than immediately killing the container.

63. What is QoS class?

Answer: A classification based on resource requests and limits.
Reasoning: Kubernetes uses QoS classes during resource pressure and eviction decisions.

64. What are the Kubernetes QoS classes?

Answer: Guaranteed, Burstable, and BestEffort.
Reasoning: They determine Pod priority under node pressure.

65. What is node affinity?

Answer: A rule that influences which nodes Pods can run on.
Reasoning: It schedules Pods based on node labels.

66. What is Pod affinity?

Answer: A rule to place Pods near other Pods.
Reasoning: It is useful when applications need low-latency communication.

67. What is Pod anti-affinity?

Answer: A rule to keep Pods apart.
Reasoning: It improves availability by spreading replicas across nodes.

68. What are taints?

Answer: Node-level restrictions that repel Pods.
Reasoning: They prevent Pods from being scheduled unless tolerated.

69. What are tolerations?

Answer: Pod settings that allow scheduling on tainted nodes.
Reasoning: Tolerations let specific Pods run on special-purpose nodes.

70. What is cordon?

Answer: Marking a node unschedulable.
Reasoning: New Pods will not be scheduled on that node.

71. What is drain?

Answer: Safely removing Pods from a node.
Reasoning: It is used before node maintenance.

72. What is a label?

Answer: A key-value pair attached to Kubernetes objects.
Reasoning: Labels help organize and select resources.

73. What is a selector?

Answer: A query used to filter objects by labels.
Reasoning: Services and Deployments use selectors to find matching Pods.

74. What is an annotation?

Answer: Metadata attached to Kubernetes objects.
Reasoning: Annotations store extra information not used for selection.

75. What is RBAC?

Answer: Role-Based Access Control.
Reasoning: It controls who can perform actions on Kubernetes resources.

76. What is a Role?

Answer: A set of permissions within a Namespace.
Reasoning: It grants access to resources in a specific Namespace.

77. What is a ClusterRole?

Answer: A cluster-wide set of permissions.
Reasoning: It can apply across all Namespaces or cluster-level resources.

78. What is RoleBinding?

Answer: It assigns a Role to users or service accounts.
Reasoning: Permissions are not active until bound.

79. What is ServiceAccount?

Answer: An identity used by Pods.
Reasoning: Applications inside Pods use ServiceAccounts to access the Kubernetes API.

80. What is NetworkPolicy?

Answer: A rule controlling Pod network traffic.
Reasoning: It restricts ingress and egress communication between Pods.

81. Why are NetworkPolicies important?

Answer: They improve security.
Reasoning: By default, many clusters allow broad Pod-to-Pod communication unless restricted.

82. What is DNS in Kubernetes?

Answer: A service discovery mechanism.
Reasoning: Pods can access Services using DNS names instead of IP addresses.

83. What is CoreDNS?

Answer: The default DNS server used in Kubernetes clusters.
Reasoning: It resolves Service and Pod DNS names.

84. What is Helm?

Answer: A package manager for Kubernetes.
Reasoning: Helm uses charts to install and manage Kubernetes applications.

85. What is a Helm chart?

Answer: A package containing Kubernetes templates.
Reasoning: It simplifies repeated deployment of applications.

86. What is a Custom Resource Definition?

Answer: A way to extend Kubernetes API.
Reasoning: CRDs allow users to define custom resource types.

87. What is an Operator?

Answer: A controller that manages applications using Kubernetes APIs.
Reasoning: Operators automate complex operational tasks like backups and upgrades.

88. What is GitOps?

Answer: Managing infrastructure and applications using Git as the source of truth.
Reasoning: Changes are applied to clusters through version-controlled repositories.

89. What is a rollout?

Answer: The process of updating application Pods.
Reasoning: Rollouts allow controlled deployment of new versions.

90. What is blue-green deployment?

Answer: Running two environments and switching traffic between them.
Reasoning: It reduces deployment risk by keeping the old version available.

91. What is canary deployment?

Answer: Releasing a new version to a small percentage of users first.
Reasoning: It allows testing in production with limited risk.

92. What is observability in Kubernetes?

Answer: Monitoring logs, metrics, and traces.
Reasoning: Observability helps understand system health and troubleshoot issues.

93. What is Prometheus used for?

Answer: Metrics collection and monitoring.
Reasoning: It is widely used to monitor Kubernetes clusters and applications.

94. What is Grafana used for?

Answer: Visualizing metrics through dashboards.
Reasoning: It helps teams understand cluster and application performance.

95. What is Fluent Bit or Fluentd used for?

Answer: Log collection and forwarding.
Reasoning: They collect logs from containers and send them to logging systems.

96. What is a PodDisruptionBudget?

Answer: A policy that limits voluntary disruptions.
Reasoning: It ensures a minimum number of Pods remain available during maintenance.

97. What is high availability in Kubernetes?

Answer: Designing the cluster and applications to remain available during failures.
Reasoning: It uses replicas, multiple nodes, load balancing, and resilient control plane components.

98. What is disaster recovery in Kubernetes?

Answer: Restoring services after major failure.
Reasoning: It requires backups, especially of etcd, persistent data, and manifests.

99. What is the most important command for debugging Pods?

Answer: kubectl describe pod <pod-name>
Reasoning: It shows events, scheduling details, container status, and errors.

100. What is the key principle behind Kubernetes?

Answer: Declarative desired state management.
Reasoning: Users declare the desired state, and Kubernetes continuously reconciles the actual state to match it.